FROM HELL TO REDEMPTION

PATRICIA MARTEN

From Hell to Redemption

Copyright © 2020 by Patricia Marten.

Paperback ISBN: 978-1-952982-01-9
Ebook ISBN: 978-1-952982-02-6

All rights reserved. No part in this book may be produced and transmitted in any form or by any means, electronic, or mechanical, including photocopying, recording, or by any information storage and retrieval system, without permission in writing from the copyright owner.

The views expressed in this work are solely those of the author and do not necessarily reflect the views of the publisher hereby disclaims any responsibility for them.

Scriptures marked KJV are taken from the KING JAMES VERSION (KJV): KING JAMES VERSION, public domain.

Published by Green Sage Agency   07/03/2020

Green Sage Agency
1-888-366-9989
inquiry@greensageagency.com

DEDICATION

This book is dedicated to my Lord and Savior Jesus Christ.

My precious Lamb of God, who has covered me with His Blood and led me on a wonderful journey. The still small voice of the Holy Spirit, who has guided me through many precarious times in my life.

For God, my one true Father, who gave His only begotten Son to redeem me.

I will praise you in the midst of the congregation, I will testify of your unconditional love that you have shown towards me. I will tell of the Faith of Jesus, for all to hear, and come to know as their own personal Savior. Praise the Lord, Amen.

TABLE OF CONTENTS

Foreword ix
Prologue xi

Chapter 1   The Growing Years 1
Chapter 2   Pornography 7
Chapter 3   A Depraved Life 11
Chapter 4   Tiamo 16
Chapter 5   The Accident 21
Chapter 6   Turmoil 24
Chapter 7   Misery 28
Chapter 8   Hardship And New Beginnings 30
Chapter 9   The Beginning Of Faith 32
Chapter 10 A New Home And A New Job 36
Chapter 11 Nova Scotia 39
Chapter 12 Faith Is Tested 44
Chapter 13 More Testing 48
Chapter 14 Heaven Sent Estate For Dogs 50
Chapter 15 Disaster 54
Chapter 16 A New Journey 58
Chapter 17 A New Life 62

FOREWORD

This book is for all those dear men, women and children out there who have suffered at the hands of men and women who want coercive control over them. May this book be a blessing to you all whatsoever you have suffered through and be inspired to know that there is indeed a light at the end of the tunnel.

A true inspirational testimony of what Jesus has done in the life of:

Patricia Marten a Lay Preacher with the Seventh Day Adventist Church.

PROLOGUE

If I had only known that the Lord was my Shepard and that Jesus loves His little children, how different might my life have been?

Knowing that we are sons and daughters of God and that He wants to lead and guide us in our lives.

How many children's lives might have been changed. Knowing that they were loved, children who longed for a hug, a tender word, had the comfort of knowing a loving parent.

Jesus says, "Come unto me, all ye that labor and are heavy laden, and I will give you rest. Take my yoke upon you, and learn of me, for I am meek and lowly in heart: and you shall find rest unto your souls. For my yoke is easy and my burden is light." Matthew 11: 28-30

Come unto Jesus, for the road I traveled in the end, was never lonely, my Savior was always with me, for, I held onto Him and never let go.

CHAPTER 1

THE GROWING YEARS

I grew up near the beautiful coast of Dublin in Ireland. There was a lot of beauty outside, however, there was darkness in the home. My earliest memories were not at all pleasant. My mother was standing at the top of thirteen stairs, with me, screaming at my father, I don't want her, you have her, catch!! My father was pleading with my mother, "Anna, put her down." Then my own voice screaming as I was thrown down the flight of stairs to my father.

My mother was a hysterical alcoholic and would continue to be like that throughout my years knowing her.

Sitting on the front steps of our house one summer, my mother said to me, "You were supposed to have been a boy, I was going to call him Patrick, I never wanted you." My name was Patricia.

My mothers' parents lived at the top of our street. This one day, when we went to visit them, I was told to sit on my grandad's knee. Oh, the horrors of what he was doing to me, unbeknown by my mother or grandmother. I started to squirm but was told to behave myself. My grandfather had his hand in my knickers and was fingering me. This sickening feeling is still with me to this day. I managed to get off of his knees and ran to a chair. My mother and grandmother scolded me and told me to get back, but I refused. I was told I deserved a good thrashing. Back at home in the kitchen, I tried to tell my mother what grandad had done to me, tears filling my eyes, but my mother rebuked me and told me again that I deserved a good thrashing.

My brother was born when I was four years old, my mother finally got her Patrick, but that was to be his middle name. I loved my brother, right from the beginning. Yes, we had our squabbles, however, that was normal for children.

When I was five years old, I kept getting sick from earache and sore throat. Unbeknown to me plans were being made regarding this.

One day, mum said that grandmother was going to take me on a bus to meet dad and that he was going to take me shopping. I used to love meeting dad and going out with him, however, when we finally got off the bus, dad wasn't there and grandmother said that he would meet us over by a large building, that was in front of us. When we reached the building, grandmother rang the bell and a nurse came out, took me by the hand and closed the door. I was on my own with this stranger, "Where is my daddy, I cried" then, as I was taken to a bed, I started screaming. I was so traumatized that I lost my voice. All these strangers around me, then I remember other children in their beds lined up to go into this big room. I had my tonsils and adenoids out.

Mum and dad came in with ice cream for me, but I couldn't talk, it would be long after I was home, before I would speak again. The trauma had so paralyzed me. Friends would come in to play snakes and ladders with me, but I couldn't talk to them. Then one day, I got out of bed and a shrill scream came out of my mouth, and I couldn't stop crying, then, I started to utter a few words.

My mother and father's marriage were not a very happy one. There would always be rows and tension at the meal table. My dad kept a carving knife by him at the table, and if I or my brother went to reach across the table to get something, we would have the carving knife slapped across our knuckles.

One day lying in bed, in the room above the living room, my mother was screaming at my father, then suddenly, I heard my father say," Anna put down that poker". Then I started screaming, thinking my mother was going to kill my dad. Dad came running into my bedroom, I was crying uncontrollably, dad came and took me in his arms and said it was alright. I kept saying, mum is going to kill you. No, Pat, everything is going to be alright. I am here, stop crying he said, as he held me tightly.

After this, I started having nightmares, where my mother was poisoning my dad. It would always be my dad that would console me. I do not however, remember my dad ever saying he loved me, nevertheless I did love my dad, however, I could only get so close to him, it was like he had a wall put up around him. Although dad would never talk about the war that he was in, I am sure he suffered from shell shock or PTSD as it is now called. I really do not know what mum felt about me, I felt sure she did not love me. It was very bewildering growing up in that house.

It is very strange, but a lot of times, I don't remember seeing my brother. It seemed just mum and me at home. If mum didn't want to see me, she would lock me up in the dark cupboard under the stairs at the back of the kitchen. This happened many times. I was terrified when this happened, I had always been very scared of the dark.

Due to the treatment from my mother, I developed stuttering and nervous shaking of my body. I was taken to a child counselor, who eventually helped me.

We had an old man come live with us from next door when his wife died. Grandad Fox as I always called him was a kind old man and I enjoyed being with him, we would play table games and he would take me out with him. This one day, Grandad Fox took my brother and me out up to the Sports Centre in Dublin, which was huge, for a walk around, this was quite a large place and quite lovely. Walking on top of a steep hill, my brother pushed me, and I fell down the hill spraining my ankle quite bad. A lady saw what happened and came up to me as she saw that I was in a lot of pain. As Grandad didn't have a car, she offered to take us all home. By the time we got home, my ankle was quite swollen, so my dad kept soaking it in cold water to try and bring the swelling down. It was going to take several weeks before the ankle was healed. My mother kept insisting that I kept walking and didn't have any sympathy for me.

My one joy growing up was when I was sent to my gran and grandpop, down on the farm. Oh, how I loved them. It was wonderful to go about without being screamed at by my mum. I always felt free as a bird when down on the farm, being with the horses and cows, helping to muck out, how I loved it. My dad's father, grandpop, was a wonderful old man, who always loved being outside, his gardens were amazing. Nan, she was so lovely and oh, her cooking, and baking, the wonderful aromas that crept from the cottage. I always felt safe there with them.

At ten years of age, I experienced my first period, I had no idea what was happening to me and was rather scared. I called my mother, who instead of being understanding, told me if I ever allowed a boy to touch me on my legs, she would kill me and throw me into the river at the end of our road.

Nothing was explained to me, I didn't know what was happening to my body. Mum gave me rags that had been torn up for me to wear, I wasn't going to get sanitary pads till the assistant headmistress at my secondary high school became involved.

It was during this time at secondary high, that I had a friend who offered to carry my books home for me. This was something new, I never had a boy offering to walk me home before, I was fourteen at the time. Well, my mother was waiting at the gate for me and was incensed when she saw me walking with a boy, she called me a whore, prostitute, all names she could think of and don't I dare ever let her see me with a boy again. It took her brother, my uncle, to intervene on my behalf, and tell her to ease up on me.

I loved to study and do homework and did well in high school and was able to go on to Wesley college for girls in Dublin, that taught the skills needed for office work, such as typing, shorthand, commerce, bookkeeping how to dress for business, and elocution classes. I enjoyed college and made a lot of friends. I passed all my exams, then, it was off to find a job.

My first job was miserable, I had a personnel officer who would continually watch me over my shoulder, which naturally made me nervous, and caused me to make mistakes. After three months, I was given my notice. Distraught at the fact of telling my parents that I had been fired, I went up to my friend's house, as I was afraid to go home. My friend, David's parents were wonderful and tried to calm me down, but obviously had to go and let my parents know. My mother was already fired up that I hadn't gone home to tell her and dad. "Did they know how scared I was to tell them, the fact that I had fled to my friend's house, where I found love?" Both mum and dad were in a storm of anger with me that I had lost my job. I was never to hear the end of it. Each day I was given the paper to scan for a job but couldn't see anything suitable. Finally, my dad spoke to a friend of his who ran a large car parts warehouse and offices, and I was offered a job in the office there. I really enjoyed the work and the girls were great, so I settled happily into this new job.

By now I was seventeen and had been out with a couple of boys, lasting anywhere up to six months, but they would soon tire of me, as I was a virgin, and intended to stay that way. One day, up at my friend David's home, we had been seeing each other for quite a while, though not truly dating, we enjoyed each other's company, going for long bike rides, and going to his parents for tea on a Sunday. One day walking me home, David asked me if I would go to bed with him? I thought, what a funny thing to ask, (I was very naive) I said alright, thinking we would just lay down for a chat or a snooze. We had never even kissed.... When the day came, and we went upstairs to his room, he started undressing, I just took my dress off and kept the rest of my clothing on and got into bed. David got in and said, "aren't you going to take your clothes off?" I said, what for? Then it hit me, I shot out of that bed, put my dress on and went home. I decided that I was not going to see him anymore.

However, that did not happen. David was my first love, even though it might have been puppy love, I really cared about David. When Sunday came around again, I went up as usual for tea. In my naivety, I had bought David a man's grooming set, hoping to appease him. He was very sulky when I saw him but decided to ignore this fact. I wasn't going to sleep with anyone before I married them and that was that.

We carried on, as usual, then one day, I ran into David all dressed up. I said, "Where are you going, all dressed up?" David said that his mum had bought it for him as they were sending him and his friend Stuart to Butlins Holiday Camp and that he would see me when he got back the following week. The following week after David was home from camp I went for tea. He and his Dad were grinning at each other. I asked what they were grinning about. I wished I hadn't. David showed me pictures that had been taken of him with a girl on his lap cuddling him. I couldn't believe it, I was devastated, they thought it was a big joke, however, I didn't and ran out of there all the way home. Hurt and feeling rejected, loss of my best friend was all I could think of.

The following week, Dad knew how upset I was, and asked me, "Would you like to come up to the club with me?" I didn't really want to go anywhere. "Come on" Dad said, it will do you good. Go and get changed and I'll take you. Arriving at the club, as we walked in through the hall, I saw a family there that we knew, who were good friends of ours. I felt easier knowing that there was someone that I knew. Dad and I sat with them and chatted as they introduced a mother and her adult son Brian and my friend Jane with her boyfriend Jim. The music started and as they got up to dance, Brian asked me to dance with him. At the end of the evening, we arranged to go out as a foursome next day.

I wish I hadn't, I wish I had given David a second chance, but I had refused to do so. How could I trust him again? Years later, I would come to deeply regret my decision not to trust David.

CHAPTER 2

PORNOGRAPHY

Brian was four years older than me. At first, I was smitten with him and obviously, I was on the rebound from David. Little did I know at the time, that this relationship would eventually destroy me.

We dated for almost a year when Brian proposed to me, he had already received my parent's blessings.

One day he drove out into the country and stopped the car on an old track.

Next, he said, I want to show you something that you haven't seen before. He undid his zip on his pants and pulled out his penis and asked me to touch it. I was appalled, I had never seen anything so ugly in my life and I shrank away from him. He didn't persist, covered himself up again and we drove home to my parents.

As you probably are aware by now, I knew nothing about sex. I did make Brian aware that there would be no intercourse between us before we were married.

The date of our wedding was arranged to be in six months' time in May, so it would be a spring wedding. My mother warned me to wait three years before having a baby.

I took a day off work to go and buy my trousseau and going away outfit for the wedding. My mother saw me walking in the town from her bus that she was on to go to work. She yelled out of the window at me to get to work and what was I doing in town? I decided to put mum out of my head so that I could enjoy my day.

I was so excited as I found everything that I needed from a beautiful pale blue suit with all the accessories to go with it, a beautiful negligee and underwear. I was so pleased I took it to Aunty Jeans' who lived a couple of doors from my parent's house. She was so pleased to see me, and when I told her what I had bought, she said, "Let us go up to Joan's room and lay it all out on the bed." She thought it all looked lovely.

I went back home to help dad get dinner ready, I had told him what I had done that day. Working on the dinner at the stove, mum suddenly burst into the house, yelling and screaming at me for not having gone to work, it was so bad, that I ran out, ran round to Aunty Jean, mum came running down the path shouting at me, don't you dare go to that woman's' house. I banged on her door, I was in such a state, that Uncle Bill her husband, said, Jean get her some brandy quick, Pat's in shock.

Our wedding night was strange, I wasn't sure if we had made love or not.

We were to fly to Spain the next day. There was a boarding house there and the people were friends of Brian's family. Instead of coming to bed with me that night, Brian stayed up to play cards with the husband. It was awful. I was very upset the lady came in with a cup of tea for me and looked at me with sympathy.

The next day, we met a couple that was staying at the boarding house, Brian was more interested in them, especially the wife then he was in me. It was not a good honeymoon.

The farmer who Brian worked for had built a house for us to live in, as he did for all his workers who got married. It was beautiful and looked out on hills and valleys from the back.

I loved to cook and bake and soon got into the way of a housewife. One day, Brian asked me to go to the newsagents and pick up a package for him. The newsagent was really put out that Brian had sent me to get it. Upon arriving home with the package. Brian opened it and showed me what was in the package, it was a book and said I want you to read this book and I will ask you questions on it tonight…

The book was all pornography, disgusting is putting it mildly. As I looked through the pages, I was so disgusted, the book was sickening. That night, he questioned me about what I had read. I felt sick, I didn't want to talk. about it. However, in the few weeks that we had been married, I had learned that I had to do what he said and not argue with him. I think Brian loved me in his own way, though he never told me.

We had been married for about three months, I wasn't feeling very well, so I went and saw the doctor, yes, I was pregnant. I was over the moon, so happy knowing that I was having a baby. When I told Brian, he too was thrilled. My parents came up that weekend for a visit. I took my dad up the garden and told him, he was delighted, however, mum had watched us from the kitchen window and when we went into the house, she flew at me and said, "Are you pregnant?" I said yes, well she screamed and yelled at me for not doing as she had said and wait the three years. I was devastated and couldn't stop crying. Poor dad, he got her out of the house and left.

This happened again when I was pregnant with my second baby, dad was pleased, and mum went into a screaming tantrum. It was horrendous.

Mum and I never spoke for five months. Dad would come up to visit me on his bike.

Life went on, my two boys were growing, how I loved them, we now had a golden retriever and the fun I would have with the dog and my two boys. I would take them and the dog and go down into the fields by the stream and we would have a lovely time. We did this a lot in the summer.

Looking back, I don't remember Brian ever playing with the boys. I always had to have the toys put away before he came home.

Then I became pregnant again, only this time Brian never acknowledge it. We were in town and I started having cramps and not feeling well. We went into a store and I knew I needed to go home, however Claude would have none of it. The next day as I rushed to the bathroom, I had clumps of blood coming out of me. I went to the doctors, who said I was mis-aborting, and to go home to bed and that the baby would take about a week to come out of me. I was so upset, knowing that I had lost a baby and especially in this way. I had been knitting, as I felt sure I was having a girl. This didn't go down well at home, Brian wasn't upset for me, he never comforted me, there was no consoling whatsoever. This did affect me terribly and I went into a deep depression.

Brian decided to have a vasectomy, therefore no more children.

The manager of the farm Brian worked on died, and understandably, Brian thought the job would go to him, unfortunately, the farmer hired someone from another farm. This did not go down well with Brian, so he started looking for jobs on other farms but to no avail. Finally, his cousin Ken from Canada suggested that we emigrate there, and Ken told Brian what we would need to do. To cut a long story short, we were accepted and a job offer from a farm in Manitoba Canada came along for him which sounded on paper very good…..When we arrived in Manitoba, that farm was not at all what we had expected, it was quite run down and the house that went with the job was unbelievable, It was filthy and in need of a lot of work, it was a total nightmare. We were supposed to have stayed there a year at least, but we left after a month. Brian's cousin Ken and his wife offered to put us up in their home in Winnipeg until Brian had a permanent job. This came quickly and we were able to move into a rented apartment. Here we stayed almost a year until we had a down payment on a house in Winnipeg.

Brian had a very good job and the pay was excellent, however, I wanted to be able to work and have an income of my own. I didn't want to go out to work yet until the boys were at least 11 years old, therefore I took in sewing and made curtains for a store in the town. Then when that came to an end, I took in typing, which helped me to have money of my own.

CHAPTER 3

A DEPRAVED LIFE

Our sex life, I cannot call it making love, because it wasn't. This was taking on a more perverse turn. I didn't like it. Brian started using play tools on me. I was changing and not for the better, I was becoming more and more repressed as if I wasn't my own person anymore. If someone asked me a question, Brian wouldn't let me answer, he would always answer for me. Our neighbors Derrick and Sue were over, and again Brian was answering for me when Derrick, who worked for social services, said to Brian, "You must stop always answering for Pat." Brian didn't much like being told he was doing anything wrong.

We didn't stay at that house long, we sold it and moved into a better part of the neighborhood. It was a lovely home. We weren't there very long when we had Derrick and Sue over again. This time, Brian said to them, "Have you ever thought of wife swapping?" Sue who was Scandinavian thought it a great idea. Without further ado, Brian took Sue by the hand and took her upstairs to the bedroom. I just looked at Derrick and couldn't stop shaking. Derrick said, "Don't worry, we will not be doing anything." Finally, it was happening, Brian wanted to be with other women, I always knew in my heart that he had been with women before he met me and most likely during the time we had been married.

One day Sue and Derrick were over, and Sue said that she had been speaking with her doctor, who she thought was very good looking, and told him about wife swapping and would he like to get involved. He said yes, so Sue invited him over to our house. Sue was going with Brian and said

I was to go with this man. He drove me to this motel, I had no idea what I was supposed to do, when he said to me, "Get undressed." He was very authoritative like Brian. I was scared, so I got undressed. It was horrible what he did to me, I felt like a cheap whore.

Brian and I were in town one day when he said to me, "I want to see you with other men." He said, "I have this magazine for wife swapping, and I want us to get involved with other couples." By this time, I had started drinking to deal with what was happening in our lives. I was becoming very repressed under his control.

My boys, what about my boys! How can this be happening? My precious sons, this isn't right! Nevertheless, I had no say in it. I knew it was wrong, so wrong. I didn't have a marriage anymore, did I ever have one, I wondered.

Brian would look up people in the magazine and get me to phone them to meet with them. Then one day he saw this advert for a party in a penthouse in Winnipeg and wanted us to go there. By now I was becoming numb to what was happening, I was not the same person. I was becoming more and more perverse, I felt like a dirty rag doll, down in the miry clay, I was losing sight of the person I used to be. Who am I, what is happening to me?

We went to the party in Winnipeg, there were quite a few people there all in a state of undress. There was a woman there that I liked, she was quiet, so when people went off with each other, I went with her. She was warm and loving and when a man came near me, I kicked him out of the way. Apparently, it was her husband, but I wanted none of it. As the evening went on, the girl went with other partners, so I had no choice.

There is a lovely mall in Winnipeg called the City Place Shopping Centre. I have visited it many times. This one time, Brian drove me and the boys there, parked the car and went inside. Suddenly he said to me, I'm just going across the road, I've been told there is a prostitute there who I would like to go and see and have that experience. I was no longer surprised at what he would come up with. The boys and I were to wait for him where we were so that he wouldn't have to go looking for us. He hadn't been gone very long when he came back and said she wasn't there.

After that, we met a couple who we became friends with and would see them nearly every week and go to this place with them that was for swingers! Then it became masochism and sadism, being hit or spanked by somebody in control of you. It was getting worse. I didn't like myself, I said to Brian, no more, I cannot go on. Then he would give me the silent treatment and just sit in his chair and sulk. It was just as hard to deal with the silent treatment, so I relented, however, I made sure I was drunk before we left to go to the swinger's club. Then one day going to this place, I became hysterical in the car and wanted to go back home, but he refused to do so. Then I tried to kill myself, I didn't want to live anymore. This would happen three more times while I was with Brian.

Then friends of ours who shared that they had gone to this place in Jamaica and said what a terrific time they had there and that we should go. Therefore, we booked up to go. I thought maybe, just maybe we can restore this marriage, so I started having fantasies about our wonderful holiday...We arrived in Jamaica and went to our room, it was quite lovely. Brian said, "I'm going to get changed and see you later." What, aren't you going to wait for me? "No, I will see you down there." I was dismayed, so I set about sorting the clothes out and got changed, when a knock came at the door, I went and opened it, there was this Jamaican who pushed through the door, pushed me to the floor and raped me. Then left as soon as he arrived, I was sick, was this all I was good for? I was heartbroken after cleaning myself up, I decided to go down and find Brian. Arriving down near the bars, I saw him, he didn't want me, he was with all these other women, they were all lined up around him. What was I to do? All my hopes just fell to pieces, I felt worthless. I went to the bar and got myself a drink. I met some people there and got talking to them and went off to a party that was being held in one of the rooms, where I met some other people, we just talked and drank, later we all decided to go down to the beach. I went off with one of them who was from New York, we hit it off straight away, and for the rest of the holiday I stayed with Jeff as Brian had taken one of the women back to our room, so I couldn't go there. I had a wonderful time with Jeff, it was truly romantic. At the end of the holiday, we had arranged to keep in touch, so had Brian with his date. I have never mentioned the rape to anybody until now.

Back in Canada, we each kept in touch with our dates. I no longer wanted Brian to touch me. Something had happened to me that gave me a new strength that I had not had before. Jeff would phone me quite often, and I arranged to fly out to New York to see him, and at the same time, Brian would go to see his new women. I was changing, I knew I could not go back to the way things were with Brian, the same went for him, he found what he wanted in this new woman. I finally told Brian that I wanted a divorce and that I was going to leave him. We had been married if you can call it that for fifteen years, the last five being in Canada.

I was working by now, however, my wage wasn't very much, and I knew I wouldn't be able to support my sons, as much as I wanted them with me therefore I agreed for Brian to have the boys if I could see them every weekend. He was not happy that I was leaving, nevertheless, I couldn't continue. I didn't know what would become of Jeff, however, I knew I had to make this break. I went to see a social worker, as I needed someone to talk to about my sons. She asked me if I had told them what was going on in the marriage. I said, "I cannot tell them, it is too horrible." The social worker after hearing what had been going on in the marriage, felt I really should speak to them. I haven't been able to bring myself to do this. The Lord willing, I pray this book will let them see the truth.

Eventually, I was to discover that Jeff was not what he proclaimed to be, this hit me quite hard, I was very vulnerable and realized this, and knew I would have to make some big changes in my life. How? I asked myself, I was terribly depressed and couldn't stop crying. I went to my doctors, who said, you either take time off work and go on holiday for a couple of weeks or I am going to put you into hospital. By this time, the divorce had gone through and I had received my half of the house sale. So, I arranged to have two weeks off work and go to Barbados which I did. Unfortunately, when I went back to work after my holiday, I no longer had the job that I was used to, it had been given to another woman. This was hard, my emotions were still taut, but I decided to strive and get on with the new work that had been allotted to me.

Brian phoned me up one day at work to see if I wanted to go for lunch, I decided to go as I didn't want to cause any waves between us in case he made it difficult for me to see my sons. Our lunch was at a striptease joint, I was disgusted. I told him that I never wanted to go to that place again.

Time went by, and Brian phoned and asked if I wanted to go for lunch, I suggested the restaurant across from where I worked. After being seated and waiting for our meals, he was looking all around at the women and girls there. Brian suddenly said to me, "All those pussies, I want to eat them all." I was so disgusted at his depravity, I got up and walked out.

I tried dating after a while, but this was not working out for me. I didn't trust men at all, I now had a distaste for them. I became very depressed and one-day while having a black Russian drink, I kept on drinking one after another and didn't want to face another day, so I decided to take a whole bottle of Tylenol and went to bed thinking that was it.

In the middle of the night, I suddenly awoke not feeling well and thought, what have I done? I called out, I don't want to die, I want to live! At this time in my life, I knew nothing of God or Jesus but God unbeknown to me, had His hand on me.

The next day I went to my doctor and told him what I had done. He scolded me and said if that was Aspirin, you would be dead, however, you are by no means out of the wars, your liver would be affected and I'm going to need to keep my eye on you for the next six months. From that time on, I did nothing but eat citrus and salads and to become healthier and fitter. I rode my bike everywhere.

CHAPTER 4

TIAMO

At work I had some good friends, these women were to have a substantial roll in my life.

Janice, one of my friends, knew I wasn't wanting to go out of a nighttime said to me, "There is going to be a fashion party and we would like you to come along. I thought that sounds safe enough, little did I know what the night would bring. I was picked up from my apartment by my friends and went to the party, which was kind of nice. When it was time to go home, we all got into the car, when I realized we were not going back to my apartment. "I said, what is going on, where are you taking me?" Janice said, "We are taking you to a nightclub, you are going to have a night out with us." Reluctantly I agreed, but said to them, "you are not to leave me on my own." Arriving there we all sat at the same table and ordered our drinks. After a while, we all got up to go and dance together. During the night while dancing, I noticed this man watching us, when we went to go and sit down, walking by him, he said, "Would you have the next slow dance with me?" Without questioning him, I said, "of course I will." What on earth was I thinking? I went and told the girls. The next slow dance was the Italian love song, Tiamo the man came up to me and said, I'm Paul, will you dance with me. He was very nice, after the dance, I went and sat with him, near the girls. I didn't want to lose sight of them. Paul and I talked, he seemed very nice. He wanted my phone number so that he could phone me, but I refused and said you can have my work number if you want and told him where I worked.

The next week, Paul phoned and asked if I would go out with him, I said no. Four times that week he phoned, each time I said no.

On the weekend, I thought to myself was I being fair, could he possibly be a decent man? So, I looked up his name in the phone book, then phoned his house. A woman answered, I said, "Does Paul live there?" she answered, yes. I said, "Oh no, he's married, he's no different to the other men." No, she said, I am his sister. Paul came on the line, and he said, "I'm not married, this is my sister, Grace." Relief flooded me, and we arranged to meet.

For three years, Paul and I dated, I didn't give him an easy time of it, as I had a hard time trusting. Paul, however, was very supportive of me. During this time, Paul arranged for me to see a psychiatrist as he knew how my so- called marriage to Brian had traumatized me. However, the psychiatrist didn't help, all he talked about was how the animals in the wild would mate. He was very odd. One day, I had a phone call from my uncle in England, to tell me that dad was dying, he had aggressive cancer. I arranged with the doctor I worked for to have time off to go to England to see my dad, he would only give me a week. Poor dad, he had gone from a robust-looking man to this thin yellow-colored man. I ran to him and hugged him, it was awful, my heart ached so much for what he was suffering. During my week with him, I told him about Paul, and he was pleased for me. The week went too fast and it was time for me to go back to Canada. I realized that I would never see my dad again. I was going to need Paul's support to help me with this.

Paul met me at the airport, and while driving home, I told him about dad and the fact that I would not see him again. Yes, I was upset. What was going to upset me, even more, was the fact that Paul had been out to a disco and met a girl that he danced with and spent time with. Right away, I could see Brian over again, oh please, not Paul too, I thought, and tears streamed down my face. When we got back to the apartment, Paul came in with my bags and put them down in the bedroom for me. Suddenly the dam burst in me, my dad and now Paul, I became hysterical and yelled at him, would I ever be able to trust him again. I tore off the necklace that I had been given and threw it at him with such a force that something broke on my dressing table. I ran out of the apartment and jumped into my car and drove. I was tearing down the road of the escarpment not caring if the car went off the road. Suddenly, it was as if my car was picked up and put in an alcove under a cliffhanging, and there I sat. A car coming towards me asked if I was alright? I numbly said, "yes." When I had gathered myself together, not knowing what had happened, or how I was on this side of the road, I drove down to the glen, switched off my car and just cried and cried. After a while, I felt the presence of a car next to mine, it was a police car, the officer came and shone his torch at me and asked what was wrong, he could see I had been crying. I relayed everything to him, he just sat and listened to me. Then after a while, he said, "I'm going to escort you out of here, and I want you to go home and get yourself a cup of tea. I thanked him for his help and promised him that I would do that.

In the meantime, Paul had been out in his car searching for me. When Paul came back, he was at a loss, he didn't know what to say, he just hugged me to him. This was 1980 and dad passed away shortly after.

Brian phoned me at the apartment and asked if I would get back with him? I said "no". Then he said, "why would you want to go out with an Italian?" then he made some crude comment. I hung up. After that he started giving me trouble about seeing the boys. Sending me letters about the boys, saying things that were not true. One was so bad that I became hysterical. I loved my boys; I knew why Brian was doing this to me. Paul read the letter and said, "I'm going to get you a lawyer and see about you getting custody of the boys." This Paul did, however, due to their age, being 15 and 16 years, they would be able to choose for themselves where they wanted to live. Eventually, they would take turns in coming to stay with me, however, never on a permanent basis.

Paul was to be the love of my life and when we married, our first dance was Tiamo.

The first six months were heaven on earth, I was so in love with Paul, I couldn't believe that a person could be so happy...However, as much as I loved Paul, things would never be quite the same again.

Six months later, Paul opened the door of our apartment and a different man came in. I said, "Paul where have you been, and what's happened to you?" I asked. Paul replied that he had been to see his psychiatrist. I thought, what has happened? Paul said I have Paranoid Bi-Polar, the doctor has signed me off work for nine months. I couldn't believe it, I knew he had problems in the past, as we had both opened to each other about our past, before, in the first year of our dating.

Everything started to change. I never knew who would be coming through the door, Jekyll or Hyde. I loved him dearly and I was determined to support him and love him. Paul's attitude started to change, sometimes he would be very aggressive other times he would be loving. However, I knew it was the illness, not the person, plus the medication that the doctor had him on took time to level out his moods.

In 1987 we bought his family's old house, that had been rented out. It was a mess, there was also an apartment upstairs that would also need a lot of work done on it. Nevertheless, I knew with the right renovation, the house and apartment would be lovely. I had previously taken a course on interior decorating and I sketched each room in the house and apartment to see what I could come up with. I knew it could be lovely with new windows, decor, and carpeting, etc.

One day during a phone call to my mother, mom had said how she needed to sell the family home and move into an apartment, however, they were all so expensive. We talked for a while then hung up. Forgetting all that I had gone through with mom, I said to Paul, "What if mum comes over here to live, dad had longed to move over to Canada, he loved it here." I said to Paul, mom could have the apartment in the house, I could decorate it to look like a cottage." Paul said, "Phone her back and ask if she would like to do that." So, I phoned mom back, and to cut a long story short, mom moved to Canada in December 1987.

By this time, we had left the apartment and were renting a small cottage across from the house, as I was working all hours of the day and night to get it ready.

How soon we forget!! Paul and I were getting excited about mom arriving just before Christmas. Paul and I went out and bought her all kinds of things that she would need in her apartment. All her bedding and curtains to match her bedspread, it was all that would lend itself to a cottage coziness.

When it was completed, it truly was lovely. We took mom shopping for the furniture that she would need so that she could move in after Christmas.

It was over Christmas that I received a call from a breeder of Golden Retrievers that I had been down to see, and, had put my name on her list for a puppy. The breeder phoned to say that my puppy was born, oh what a lovely Christmas present, and I was invited to go there and see the puppies after Christmas.

In the new year, the house was finished, and it was truly lovely, and we all moved in. Mom in her apartment and Paul and I in the house, plus our new addition, Sandy my puppy. We were very happy there, for a while?

Mom started to cause trouble between Paul and me. She would yell at him, which didn't help Paul at all, nor myself. Mom made it clear that she didn't like Paul. Neither Paul nor I needed this kind of trouble with mom.

When I cleaned the oven (it was self-clean), I would open the windows during the cleaning process. Mom phoned down, yelling at me through the phone, "Are you trying to kill me? What's that smell?" This was just the start of our problems with mom.

Paul started to get in trouble with the police due to threatening people. One day, I asked my pastor from the Lutheran church where we were married, if he could pay me a visit while Paul was at work. This he did, and while telling him what was happening with Paul, I received a phone call from Paul's workmate to say the police were waiting for Paul at GM, apparently, Paul had gone to the house of one of the men at GM and threatened his wife. Why was he doing this, I thought to myself. Then I relayed what was happening to the pastor. "Was it the Bi-polar disorder that he has, that has caused all this, I was becoming distraught with all these violent episodes.

Paul was remanded on bail, till the court hearing.

CHAPTER 5

THE ACCIDENT

January 1989, it was a beautiful day, I was on my way home to mom from work to have lunch with her, as I usually did. I would get Sandy my Retriever, let her out in the garden, then take her up to mom's apartment. Only this day I never reached home.

Driving along towards the stoplights, my light was green, cars were lined up on the other road at the stop sign, there was nothing towards my left, so I proceeded across when out of my eye I saw this car careening on to me, I just remembered screaming, when everything turned black.

Next, I remember coming to, in the hospital in a lot of pain, wondering where was I, what had happened? Due to my head bouncing off of my window, I had sustained a brain injury, that would leave me with horrendous headaches, unable to speak properly, loss of memory, not of my family though, but of things that I should know. Severe back injury, where I was unable to walk without the use of a stick. My Sandy, if I needed to go to the bathroom, would grab hold of my dressing gown and take me to the bathroom, sit and wait for me, then take me back again. Sandy was to be my saving grace. I loved to read but couldn't remember what I had read. I had lost the ability to write, all I could do was scribble. I would have to teach myself how to do the alphabet. When will I be normal again, I thought to myself? The intense pain in my head, back and body, nothing the Neurologist had given me was helping. Thinking to myself, I will overcome this, I will write again. Gradually after time, I would copy from a book onto paper to help me write. It was so hard as my hands, especially the left hand and arm was causing me problems from nerve damage.

Back and forth to the doctors, it was very hard and frustrating.

Paul bought me a tape recorder to help me. Taking a book, I proceeded to read and re-read the book out loud into the recorder. Even though I couldn't remember the context of what I was reading. Gradually after several months of doing this my speech started to sound more fluent. During this time, I started copying down words and practicing the alphabet, large and small letters, and gradually over time the letters started to get better, then copying out sentences from the book. It wasn't perfect, but it was a great improvement. Now, what am I going to do about my memory I thought to myself. "I cannot seem to remember things, that I have been told," I said to Paul, then he said, "Why don't you write down things you have been told." So, I started to do this. This took a lot of effort and discipline and lots of tears of frustration were shed. Nevertheless, slowly, painfully slowly, I started to remember enough to get by with. This was now ten months after the accident. I know it was very frustrating for Paul, however, he knew this accident would be bringing in money, and he was looking at the dollar signs. There were many visits to the lawyers, and counseling, as well as visits to the doctors for the insurance company. The visit to McMaster University to see a Neurologist. So many tests were done, it became completely overwhelming. This would be going on for the most part of a year.

Paul took me out to buy another car, as my car was destroyed. My counselor had to take me out in the car to help me relax while driving. Every time I came, to a green light I would draw to a stop, I was afraid to proceed. This too took a lot of time as I had lost my confidence in driving.

December 1989 came and I was determined that I would work again, ignoring the Neurologist advice about never trying to work again, his words still echoed in my ears, "You will never be academic again, you will have to get used to the idea of staying at home." I was determined to prove him wrong. I will fight this, I will go back to work again, no one will stop me. I will prove to them that I am able to work.

How am I going to do this, I thought to myself? I need to do something to help my memory and I need to take control of my speech and be able to write again properly. These thoughts kept running through my mind.

I will do this, I will succeed. I had come a long way; however, I still have a long haul in front of me, but I will do it.

One day, scanning the newspaper for a job opportunity, there was an advertisement for a seminar to be held at one of the motels in town for work in the insurance field. I thought about this and felt a surge of excitement swell up in me. I would go along.

The seminar was very interesting, and I felt this was something I would like to do. By now my speech was pretty good, plus I would work on it more. My writing had come along, although I would have to work at this throughout my life. I remembered nothing about grammar, etc. this too would be a continuous learning lesson throughout my life. My memory was still not good. I still couldn't recount what had been said to me, even to this day. My short-term memory was bad, however, this too I would try and conquer to the best of my ability.

I phoned the insurance company and asked for an interview, which I received for the next day. When I went for the interview, I didn't hold anything back, I told the manager about my head injury and that I had a problem with my memory, nevertheless, I was willing to learn. The manager told me that I would have to pass an exam before I could start, but that they would work with me and give me all the help that I would need. I was thrilled. The manager gave me books to study at home and when I was ready, he would give me test papers to see how I was doing. This he did. I failed the first exam, almost passed the second exam, and was told I would have to wait six months to try again. I said to the manager, "What if I wrote a letter to the insurance board and told them of my head injury and ask them if I could be allowed to take the exam again?"

The manager agreed to this and a letter was sent off. A new exam date was given to me, this time I passed. I was exhilarated. The year had been long and hard and finally I felt I had overcome all odds.

The work was enjoyable, and I excelled in it. I started to earn a lot of money, it was mind-boggling to me, however, it was long hours, from early morning to late at night. There was a new strength and enthusiasm developing in me.

CHAPTER 6

TURMOIL

Every Thursday, Paul and I would go to his mom and dad for supper, which I loved. I also loved them a great deal they were wonderful to me. This one evening while at supper, I was saying where I had to go for insurance business that night. Paul's dad said, "You shouldn't be driving around in the nighttime, it isn't safe, there was a car-jacking up at the lights." So, with that in mind, when I went out that night, I was careful to lock my car doors while driving around. This night would take me to a home in an unsavory part of Winnipeg. The numbers on the homes were not very clear, so I parked my car and started to walk up the street. Suddenly this Shepherd was beside me, then disappearing, then back again. When I arrived at the house, the dog was with me, the woman answering the door, said I must ring the humane society about that dog. I was with her for two hours, when I came back out, the dog was waiting for me. Again, he disappeared, as I walked back towards my car. Opening my car, which was a two-door, I got in and felt a presence in the car, I looked back, and there was the Shepherd on my backseat. To this day, I never knew how he could have got in. I thought to myself, I'll drive down to the office and phone the humane society and find out if anyone has lost this dog. No record of it was found, so the man at the society said: "If you give us your address, we will pick the dog up tomorrow for you." I just said, "thank you," and hung up, this dog was going to get a new home.

Paul was just leaving for his night shift when I arrived home with the dog. I told him what had happened, Paul was thrilled, his name was going to be Mickey. Not wanting to bring a strange dog into Sandy, I let her out into the garden to see what would happen, you would think they had known each other, running around the garden together, then coming into the house. Not knowing the personality of Mickey, I thought for the night, I'll let him sleep in the basement, well when I opened the door, and Mickey saw the stairs, I have never seen such fear in a dog's eyes, it was awful. I closed the door, gave him a brush and something to eat and drink then went into the bedroom where Sandy was asleep on the bed. I thought to myself, I'll just see what Mickey does. I got myself ready for bed and climbed in, Mickey came and laid by the side of my bed, and there he was still in the morning.

I noticed Mickey was very thin, so I knew he would need building up. Mickey would be accompanying me on my travels whenever I went to work, of a night-time, he was now my guard dog, and he loved it.

I was still suffering from back pain and headaches and was put in touch with a therapist who I was to see on a regular basis. The therapy helped at the time, however, it would not last, I was in constant pain.

Paul was very good at taking me to see other doctors, nevertheless, our life at home was not so good. I would always be home to cook dinner, which was usually three courses. However, before I had completed my meal, Paul had finished and was up from the table saying, "I'm going to take a shower, as I'm going out." This happened every night, he would shower and get dressed up and go out, never saying where he was going, and would most often arrive home between 2 am and 4 am. Never saying where he had been.

I felt Paul and I were drifting apart, so I spoke to him and suggested that we have a lunch date once a week. Unfortunately, that didn't help, sitting at the table in the restaurant felt like sitting with a stranger, it became more and more uncomfortable. Then the threatening started, and Paul started to become violent towards me.

Then about six months into my job, things began to be intolerable at home. Paul would start threatening me and saying, "You wouldn't dare leave me." Sneering at me as he said this. For some time, he had been talking about the Mafia, which was prevalent in Winnipeg. I had never taken him seriously, but now I was beginning to wonder what was going on?

Paul hadn't wanted to be with me to make love for some time. I had bought beautiful nightwear to entice him, nothing worked. I would go to bed in tears and cuddle up with Sandy and Mickey. People in the neighborhood started talking about seeing him with other men. I thought to myself, is this why he doesn't want me anymore?

Paul started threatening me more and more, the stress, I couldn't deal with it, I was becoming sick again, the pains were getting worse. So, I went to see my lawyer that I had for my accident. Ted said, "I'm going to send you upstairs to a woman lawyer who will advise you what to do. Ted phoned the lawyer who said she would see me, so up I went to see her. Jill was very nice, I felt comfortable with her. I told her all that was happening between me and Paul, the way he would threaten me, his possibly going with other men, our lack of money to pay for things, taking out loans with both our names on it. Where was the money going? Recently I had noticed that Paul had all kinds of credit cards, for what? During our conversation, I told Jill that I was becoming more and more scared of Paul. This wasn't the man I had married. We had been married for seven years, yes, I still loved him, but I feared him now.

Jill advised me to move out of the house, "Do you have anyone to help you?" she asked me. "Yes, I could ask my sons if they would help." Then Jill said, "I will get the separation papers drawn up for you. I phoned John my eldest son to see if he and Ken would help me. We arranged that they would come down with a U-Haul truck on Saturday morning. While Paul was out that night, I started sorting and packing what I would need. I hadn't thought about where I would live. Paul was out when my sons arrived, who came in with their girlfriends to help me pack. I was going to take half the furniture and leave the rest for Paul.

Paul came back early and came into the house and asked me what was going on. I was crying and said to Paul that I was going to leave him and that I could no longer deal with what was happening in our lives. This completely broke my heart, I loved him so much. Paul went around to tell his mom and dad.

I had nowhere to go. I phoned a real estate person I knew, to ask if he knew of any apartments available where I could go, explaining that I needed to get out of my home that day. He asked me to go and meet him and he would see what he could do. Taking my checkbook with me I met him at his office, I knew I looked a mess, but that couldn't be helped. The agent said he had phoned a couple of men he knew, and they had an apartment that I could move in to. Meeting with the two men, I arranged to move in that day. I paid them a month's rent and they gave me the key.

Driving back home to help my sons, I met with chaos. Paul's mum and dad were there accusing me of leaving their son who was sick. They didn't care that I too was unwell and on the verge of a nervous breakdown. It was awful because I had loved them so much. Next, I had to go to my mom and tell her that I would be in touch with her. By this time, I was hysterical.

My sons and their girlfriends helped me to move into the apartment with Sandy and Mickey. I was safe for a while…….

CHAPTER 7

MISERY

One day coming in from work, there was a message on my phone, it was from Paul, Oh the horror of it, the message said, "I know where you are, I'll get you, you pig."

I took the tape out of the recording and went down to the police station and made a report. They said that they would bring Paul in for questioning and would keep an eye on the place where I lived.

I knew I had to get out of where I was living in Winnipeg, so I started scanning the newspaper for a place where I would feel safe. There was a house for rent in Minnedosa. I phoned mom and asked her if she wanted to move out of the apartment and come and live with me in Minnedosa, she said that she would, so I said to her, "We could split the rent between us." I'll make arrangements to come and view the house and call you back.

Mom and I rented the house and my sons, and their girlfriends helped us to move in along with the help of mutual friends of ours. This went smoothly. Mom had her little BijonFrise, Benji, who, I had bought for her for Mother's Day the previous year. Sandy and Mickey and Benji all got along famously and had a nice big garden to play in. Mom and I settled into the new home. All was well....

By now I had left the first job in Winnipeg and had a new job with another insurance company close to Minnedosa. At first, it was great, I liked the people I was working with. However, things weren't so great at home!

Mom would be drinking throughout the day and would shout at me when I arrived home from work, saying she was not my skivvy. What was she talking about? In the beginning, mom would get a start on dinner for me, but now she just wanted to sit and watch the TV with her glass of brandy. So, I would prepare and cook dinner for us. I didn't want any arguments with her. Mom had her own sitting room and a separate bedroom. Which was good, nevertheless, mom was getting bad-tempered again. One day, I was offered the chance to move into a lovely bungalow with cheaper rent, that was further into the village, this would be much better for both of us. Well, mum yelled and screamed at me that she was not moving. I went to speak to a mutual friend of ours to see if they could help persuade mum and let her see that it would be much more beneficial for us to move. There was a lovely big garden for the dogs, also there was a garage at this place, which would be more secure, as I had trouble with my tires being burst where we lived, plus Paul and his family had been seen driving by the house and the police had been involved again.

We moved into the new bungalow, it was truly lovely and cozier than the first place. The downstairs of the bungalow was finished and carpeted throughout. Again, mom had her own sitting room and bedroom. However, things were not good between us, plus I was getting stressed out and having a hard time with my job, which I was finding more and more difficult.

One day driving to work, I didn't know where I was. I stopped the car and tried to figure out what was happening to me. I thought to myself if I drive back and follow the road in the opposite direction, I might be able to get back home. This I eventually did. Upon reaching home, I phoned my doctor and told him what had happened. The doctor said, "I want to see you in my office today." I managed to reach the doctor's office and upon seeing him and talking, he said to me, "You've had a mental breakdown, I am signing you off of work for six months." What would I do, where would the money come from to pay the bills? Finally, I was sent to meet with trustees to discuss if I should claim bankruptcy. They were very helpful; they knew about Paul and that I was fearful of meeting him. They said that they would look after me. So, I became bankrupt and everything ceased. It was an awful time. I did receive a long- term disability payment that had been long overdue, that helped mom and me out for a while.

CHAPTER 8

HARDSHIP AND NEW BEGINNINGS

Now, three years later, I was suffering from a second nervous breakdown. Having tried to work and not having the capabilities to do the work given me, plus my marriage breakdown and subsequent divorce, and the bankruptcy, on top of everything, Things were becoming so hard to handle, I didn't know what to do anymore.

So, here was I in bed, wracked with continual pain in my head and in my body. Crying against my pillow. As I looked toward the books on my bedroom shelf, my eye caught hold of a book, slowly getting out of bed, I went and picked up the book, it was my old school Bible. Suddenly a need surged through me, getting back into bed, I opened the Bible, and there before me was Psalm 23 that called to me…The Lord is my Shepherd, I shall not want. He maketh me to lie down in green pastures: He leadeth me beside the still waters. He restoreth my soul: He leadeth me in the paths of righteousness for His name's sake. Yea, though I walk through the valley of the shadow of death, I will fear no evil: for thou art with me: thy rod and staff they comfort me. Thou preparest a table before me in the presence of mine enemies: Thou anointed my head with oil; my cup runneth over. Surely goodness and mercy shall follow me all the days of my life: and I will dwell in the house of the Lord forever…As I read it, tears ran down my face. Then reading it repeatedly again, now seeing the Lord holding my hand as I was led through the Psalm. Laying me down gently on the green pastures, then leading me beside the still waters. This was soothing to my heart and soul.

In January, six months later, having obtained work in an office of a large garden nursery. Trying to overcome my inability to do the job that I was assigned to do. The owner of the nursery, who was also the president of the Full Gospel Businessmen's Fellowship International (FGBMFI), asked me if I would like to type out the schedules of the upcoming speakers for the monthly meetings, this would include their testimonies. This I was pleased to do, and gradually over time the testimonies started working on me, and I asked if I could possibly go to these meetings. The owner was thrilled as no one from the office had asked if they could attend the meetings before this time. It was agreed that I would go the following Monday and that I should sit at his family's table.

This was to be the beginning of a long journey that I would take with the Lord...At the meeting, on Monday, I was enthralled with the testimonies and the hymns that were sung. At the end of the evening, people were invited to go forward to accept Jesus into their lives...As I sat in my chair, something was happening, I found myself getting up and going forward...The President asked me if I wanted to accept Jesus into my life...All of a sudden tears started streaming down my face, and I knew without a doubt, Yes, I wanted Jesus to come in and take over my heart, and be in charge of my life.

Now, as I walked out of that meeting, I knew for sure that I was no longer the same person that had walked into that meeting earlier in the evening.

Something so wonderful had changed in my life, I felt lighter and for the first time in years, I felt happy. I was experiencing perfect joy, knowing that I was no longer alone and was truly loved. As I drove home, the hymns and songs that we had been singing came to me, and I started singing them...Arriving home, I greeted my dogs with such joy. Letting them have a run outside, the dogs and I went to bed. Opening my Bible to Matthew, an understanding was coming to me of what I was reading, the Holy Spirit was teaching me. I was so hungry for the Word of God and holding on to every word that I read. Finally putting the Bible down at 3 in the morning, I went peacefully to sleep.

CHAPTER 9

THE BEGINNING OF FAITH

A few weeks later, at work, the manager gave me a letter, saying that they were not going to renew my contract and that I was to leave in two weeks. I was devastated, how would I pay my rent? Arriving at home that night, I collapsed in tears on the kitchen floor, crying out to the Lord for help. Suddenly a feeling of a warm blanket put around me, then a still small voice, saying, "you must write out your testimony and give a copy tomorrow at work to the owner and the manager." Oh, how am I going to do this I cried? The still small voice said, "I will help you."

Sitting down on my couch with pad and pencil, I started to write, yet, it wasn't me writing, the words were flowing from the pencil to the pad through the help of the Holy Spirit. By being obedient to the Lord and handing a copy to the manager and owner in the morning and feeling rather flustered by it, saying that the Lord had directed me to do this, they each understood... This obedience and the beginning of faith in the Lord resulted in the manager and owner giving me two months to look for a job instead of two weeks. "Praise the Lord."

By now I was living in a small summer cottage, that had no insulation in the house whatsoever, and walls that you could see being moved by the wind outside. Winter in Manitoba Canada is cold...Even my beloved dogs, Sandy my Golden Retriever and Mickey my Shepherd, who had been with her all these years, did not like lying on the thin carpet on the floor with ice underneath it, which would crunch when I walked on it. It was so cold there, and one day everything froze up in the house. There was no water as the pipes had frozen up. I was four days without water, it was no fun. I had the oven on and open, to try and get heat. The wall heater didn't give out much heat that was in the living room. The only place that we could be warm was upstairs and in bed, curling up together. I would lay in bed and listen to the rats and mice running between the walls.

One day, Mickey was in the other bedroom across from mine and was playing with something, I went over to investigate, I wasn't sure if it was a large mouse or small rat, it was dead. Oh, what am I going to do, I don't like this; I grabbed it by the tail, and ran down the stairs, freaking, Oh, I don't like this, Oh, I don't like this, and flushed it down the toilet fast.

Each day I would pray to the Lord, "Father when my settlement comes in, all I want is a little house in the country that is warm, with a garden for my dogs, and your beautiful trees around."

> Mark 11:24-25 Therefore I say unto you, what things so ever ye desire when ye pray, believe that ye receive them, and ye shall have them. And when ye stand praying, forgive, if ye have ought against any: that your Father which is in heaven may forgive you your trespasses.

During the time living at the cottage, my friend Ellen invited me to supper and to go afterward on the candlelight parade that is held every Christmas. They had invited a friend of Ellen's husband John, to dinner as well. Mike was in the army based in Winnipeg where John use to be before his retirement. The evening was lovely, and we all had a really good time.

Mike invited me out for a meal with him the following week. He seemed very nice and was a gentleman towards me. However, I made it clear that there would not be a relationship, just a friendship. We would meet for a game of cards or just to go for a walk with the dogs. Nevertheless, over the course of a few months, Mike started talking about taking me on a holiday, as he talked about the holiday, and about staying in a motel, I said, "we would need separate rooms," Mike said, "what for? I'm not paying for two rooms when we can share a room." I said, "there is no way I am sharing a room with you." He became persistent; however, I refused the idea. Then whenever I saw him after this, he started pushing himself towards me, trying to put his arms around me. This was not what I wanted. When he had left, I prayed to the Lord, "Father something is not right about the friendship I have with Mike," and as I prayed, I was seeing a black spot in regard to Mike, so I decided to end the friendship. My friends Ellen and John were not happy with me, saying, that I had hurt their friend. Nevertheless, as far as I was concerned it was ended.

Thankfully, I was able to get mom into a seniors apartment before all this happened, and she was comfortable there and happier, as she was in a small town center, the apartment was behind all the shops that she would need for her purposes. Mom liked to shop; she was never happy in the country setting. Besides all this, mom had people her own age around her.

During the last two months of my work at the nursery, I didn't go to work this particular Wednesday, I was in so much pain with my back. Laying there resting, the phone rang, upon answering it, I was shocked to find it was Paul on the phone. I said, "how did you know where I was?" Paul answered, and said, "I asked the operator for your number." Still shocked, I prayed quickly and realized this had to be the Lord's intervention, as normally I wouldn't have been home. So, I related to Paul about receiving the Lord into my heart and all that the Lord has been doing for me. I told him about the monthly meetings on Monday's that I go to, at the FGBMFI. Paul said, "I would like to go to one of those meetings," so I told him when the next meeting was going to be, and where it was held, it was going to be on the Monday coming. I asked him how he was? Paul said he missed the dogs. So again, I prayed quickly, then said, "would you like to meet the dogs and me at the park on Saturday?" Paul said, "he would." So, we arranged a time to meet.

That Saturday, I met Paul with my dogs, Sandy and Mickey, having decided to share what I knew about Jesus my Lord and Savior. I had been attending a Full Gospel Church since accepting Jesus into my life. I was so hungry for the Word of God and what it meant to me in my life. I knew I still loved Paul, that kind of love just doesn't die. I was now determined to reach Paul for Jesus. The Lord had His plans for Paul if only Paul would surrender himself to the Lord. We spent an hour walking the dogs, then Paul left promising that he would meet me on Monday at the FGBMFI meeting.

Paul met me that Monday and enjoyed the meeting, obviously, it was going to take some time for Paul to accept the Lord. Paul is Catholic and will not do anything that is against what his parents want, except that they never knew that Paul and I met to walk the dogs each Saturday and that we would continue to do so for quite a while. During this time, Paul had bought himself a Bible. I had hoped that we would be able to study together, however that never happened. Paul would only give me an hour each Saturday.

The men from the FGBMFI wanted to meet with Paul for a coffee and talk, to be able to help him and reach him for Jesus. When one of the men, phoned Paul's home where he was living with his parents, Paul's mom answered the phone and wanted to know what they wanted with her son. When they said that they wanted to go for a coffee with Paul, she got angry with them. Paul would never call them back. He wouldn't do anything to go against his parent's wishes.

CHAPTER 10

A NEW HOME AND A NEW JOB

It was now four years since the accident and my lawyer phoned to say, "I am expecting your settlement cheque to come in, very soon, start looking for your house." This I did with the help of an agent, who took me to see a certain home. It was along a country lane, the home looked like a cottage, tucked in between tall pine trees. The Inside of the home was so lovely and warm, two bedrooms, a living room, a beautiful eat-in kitchen, the bathroom beautifully done, then down a few stairs to a stone-paved sunroom looking out onto a lovely garden with fruit trees and the most beautiful weeping birches.

As I was leaving to get into the car, the Lord stopped me, and said, "take a look around." I gasped, my prayer to the Lord, He was answering it. It was the little house in the country, with a garden for my dogs. "Oh Lord, this is exactly what I had prayed for, look at all those beautiful trees." Excited, I said to my agent, "I'm going to make an offer." After going back and forth a few times, we all came to an agreement. I was overjoyed and couldn't stop praising the Lord. Father, how faithful you are to me.

I now had a new job; I was working in the administration of a large store chain in the center of Winnipeg It had taken a while to get used to the job, but I enjoyed the work. Yes, it was tiring and stressful, but I was determined to make a go of it and succeed.

After getting settled into my new home, I saw that there was a Calvary Church down at the end of the road from my home, so I decided that I would start attending. The teaching was so much better here than at my previous church and I was learning so much. I became involved with the large choir there, Oh, it was wonderful, how I enjoyed this. The choir director was amazing and made the practice sessions so enjoyable. I was so very happy here at this church, I felt settled.

However, at work was a different story, I was put under a lot of stress again and eventually became ill. I went to see my doctor who said no work for two weeks. The very next day, my supervisor phoned me and said I was to come straight into work. Of course, I was not able to. Every day, she would phone me and order me into work. Every day, I was in a flood of tears and became even sicker. I went to see my doctor again, who put me in the care of a consultant, who told me that I would have to stop working, my nervous system and my body was breaking down, and that this would get worse unless I listened to advice. Therefore, with the help of the consultant, I was able to go on disability. The consultant wrote to my work with a report of my illness. Then I received a letter from my supervisor who accused me of job abandonment. This letter I sent to my lawyer telling him what was happening. I was advised to call Human Resources at head- office of the investment firm that I worked for. I did this, and they took care of the problem for me.

Then one day after a bad dizzy spell, I laid down and cried out to the Lord, "Father, what do you want me to do?" The still small voice came back to me, "I want you to sell this home." "Oh, Lord," I cried out to Him, "this beautiful home You gave me...However, Father, You gave it to me, and You can take it away again...please Father, give me confirmation in the morning, fill me with your song and Word."

The next morning, as I woke up, I felt different, there was no foreboding about leaving this home, where I had been for the last two years, I had a sense that the Lord was leading me in a different direction, that He was in charge. I couldn't stop praising the Lord, He filled me with confirmation with His Word, and I was singing songs of praises, glorifying my God. I next phoned a Christian estate agent that I knew and told him that the

Lord was asking me to sell my home. He said he would pray about it and get back to me.

> Jeremiah 29:11-14 For I know the thoughts that I think toward you, saith the Lord, thoughts of peace, and not of evil, to give you an expected end. Then shall ye call upon me, and I will hearken unto you. And ye shall seek me and find me when ye shall search for me with all your heart. And I will, be found of you, saith the Lord.

CHAPTER 11

NOVA SCOTIA

As the weeks and months went by, I was still very unwell, however, I had been journaling what the Lord was telling me, and the scriptures He was giving me, as I spent each day with Him in His Word...One day, I asked the Lord, "Father, where are you sending me?" I will need a new home to go to...suddenly, the still small voice said, "I am sending you to Nova Scotia." I suddenly realized what the Lord was doing for me. I had been heartbroken so many times over my sons.

Remembering suddenly their weddings and how they had broken my heart. How my younger son had led me to believe he wanted photos' of when he was a baby for himself, and I willingly had given him some photos' that I had. Sitting at his wedding reception with my uncle, cousin and my mom. Seeing the photos' that I had given him being portrayed of him on a screen as a baby, with his dad, I wasn't included, it was as if I hadn't been there when he was a baby. I had made all the gifts for the guests, which had taken ages to do. Even the makeup for his wife for her wedding day. I loved her as my own daughter, it was as if I had never existed. I was so glad my uncle was there, he could see how hurt I was, he was the one that comforted me. I wish I had never gone to that wedding.

My elder son was getting married, I was so excited about his wedding. This was when I was seeing Paul again. I wanted to bring Paul, however, my son said Paul could not go to his wedding, so I went with my younger son and his wife. At the reception, I. was to regret ever having gone. I was sitting at a single table up in front with my younger son and his wife, however, they didn't stay with me, I was left on my own, while they went and sat with members and friends of the family. When the dancing started, not once did my elder son ask me to dance with him, although he danced with others, he ignored me the whole time. I couldn't stop tears coming into my eyes, but I refused to let them flow. Again, I wished I had never gone to the wedding. I couldn't leave as my younger son and his wife had brought me. How could my son's do this to me? These weddings had put me through too much stress, how would I ever overcome this?

Knowing that my elder son would come down to visit relatives around the corner from where I lived, yet, not come to see me, hurt me very much. If I went up to visit with my younger son and his wife, Brian would be there with his wife on many of the occasions it was more than I could handle.

So much grief was my Lord taking me away from or was this the fact that I would be going on a journey with Him that would either weaken me or strengthen me in my faith with my Father. Little did I know what horrors were awaiting me ahead.

Now, back to Nova Scotia where I had been once before with Sandy and Mickey for a wonderful two- week holiday in a bed and breakfast. Now, getting out the map of Nova Scotia on the south shore, where I had previously been, and remembering the prayer I had uttered to the Lord walking along the beautiful sandy beach with my dogs. "Oh Lord, I pray that you will bring me back here when I am retired, it is so beautiful and peaceful here." Little did I know at the time, the Lord was going to answer my prayer far sooner than I had expected. Now, looking at Nova Scotia on the map, I prayed, "Father, where are you going to send me?" As I looked at the map, the Lord lifted my eyes up to the northern part, suddenly I burst out, what's up there Lord? My eyes were resting on the Northumberland Strait, way at the top of Nova Scotia.

The Lord was asking me to leave my past and my family behind and was going to start something new in my life. "Oh Father" I prayed; I will follow You wherever You want me to go. God was going to be taking me away from all the grief I had experienced. Brian: Paul and his family who were hungry for my settlement. My son's whom I loved, who had broken my heart. Her mother who thought she should get the settlement. All the ugliness, God was going to put behind her.

Making arrangements with my agent, to get in touch with an agent in Nova Scotia for me to view some homes. This he did for me and the following day I received a call from the agent in Nova Scotia and we agreed that I would fly out there to meet her and view some homes. The night before I was to meet the agent, I prayed, "Lord, you show me the house you want me to have, make it loud and clear for me so that I know for sure. Be my constant guide as I want to be where you want me to be, not where I want to be, for you alone, know what is best for me, thank you Father, Amen."

This was October 1995...Flying out to meet with the agent, who said upon my arriving, "I have six homes to show you. So off we went. The Lord wasn't in any of the houses...However, as we started up a certain country road, I suddenly said to the agent, "that's the house, over there," she looked at me strangely, and as we went up the driveway, I knew this was the house. Going to the back door and climbing up the stairs, opening the door into the kitchen, the Lord was letting me know, loud and clear, and before I saw the rest of the house, I said, "I'm putting in an offer...The Lord had given me bigger and even better than I could imagine, so many trees, and woods on twenty-two acres of property.

Back in Manitoba again, there were no offers on my home. By April 1996, the six-month contract that I had on the home in Nova Scotia was up. However, I somehow knew that I would be in Nova Scotia by the end of August of that year.

During this time, I phoned Ellen my friend, who I hadn't seen since I stopped seeing Mike, and asked her if she wanted to come around for a visit and a cup of tea. This she agreed to. While talking with Ellen, she mentioned that Mike was not in a good position and badly needed friends and that he had been back in Winnipeg for some time. As Ellen was talking to me about his situation, I felt compassion for him welling up in me. So, I said to Ellen, "do you think he would like me to write to him?" However, I said I did not have his address. Ellen said, "I think he would appreciate hearing from you." I will get the address for you. This she did.

A week after I had written to Mike, I received a phone call from him, saying how pleased and surprised he was to hear from me. We talked for a while, and I said we should keep in touch, which we did, most days, talking to each other. Mike knew I wasn't well and that I wasn't getting any better. Due to my physical and mental incapacity, I was having a hard time getting organized. I preferred to spend time with the Lord journaling and reading His scriptures and walking my dogs.

In June that year, Mike said that he wanted to marry me and take care of me. I really didn't want to get married again, however, I was needy, and knew I needed someone to help and look after me. Mike said that he would send a ticket for me to fly out to where he was living in Winnipeg and that we would be engaged. I arranged for a local kennel to look after my dogs for me for a few days. Mike and I became engaged but didn't know when to plan the wedding. "Mike," I said, I truly believe my home will be sold in August and that I will be in Nova Scotia by the last day of August. I had such a strong conviction that the Lord was going to be moving things along for me. Mike, however, didn't have this conviction, but I was sure.

In the second week of August that year, I had an offer come in on the house. It was very low, so I took it to the Lord and asked, what was I to do? Again, the still small voice said…Give unto others who have less than you, therefore, I accepted the offer. I then contacted the agent in Nova Scotia and asked, if the house was still available? It was, so I went in with a lower offer, it was accepted. I was in Nova Scotia on the last day of August, that year. Mike had driven down to help me pack and move me and the dogs out to Nova Scotia.

> Isaiah 40:31 But they that wait upon the Lord shall renew their strength; they shall mount up with wings as eagles; they shall run, and not be weary, and they shall walk and not faint.

We arranged to get married in September that year and I asked my friends to be my bridesmaid and maid of honor, this they agreed to and would fly out to be with me prior to, and after the wedding. Mike and I were going to spend our wedding night at a local bed and breakfast…Little did I know that my nightmare was about to begin.

> Psalm 146:3 Put not your trust in princes, nor in the son of man, in whom there is no help.

The good Lord never promised to heal me, I still suffer to this day, from the injuries, compounded by other injuries incurred in the next part of my story. I now know my limitations and am not worried.

Jesus has seen me through and has promised never to leave me or forsake me, He is with me always and will continue to be with me through the horrors still to come in my life. I am and have been on an exciting and fulfilling journey with my Savior and my Forever Friend.

CHAPTER 12

FAITH IS TESTED

As I arrived in Nova Scotia, little did I realize that from 1996, when I arrived, to 2005, my faith in the Lord was going to be seriously tested? I had no idea that I would be traveling through the valley of the shadow of death with my Shepherd.

Unfortunately, I didn't know to whom I had married. It had not been a marriage of love, but of convenience. As the weeks and months went by, it was like being on a roller coaster. The coercive control, it was like a recap of my marriage to Brian, having to be compliant and willing to please. The physical and mental stress became much worse. Mike was perverse in the way he treated me, not as a husband should treat his wife, his sexual abuse and rape were continuous. I would be in bed asleep, when I would feel hands around my neck in a stranglehold then raping me, then pulling my hair back tight and raping me again. I couldn't move for fear had engulfed me. I would never see his face when Mike did this as he always came from behind me. Our marriage was a sham. I ended up having panic attacks every time he came near me. Things had gone from bad to worse. How was I going to cope with this…O Father, I need your help and advice?"

> 1Peter 1:7 and 13, That the trial of your faith, being much more precious than of gold that perisheth, though it be tried with fire, might be found unto praise and honor and glory at the appearing of Jesus Christ. 13. Wherefore gird up the loins of your mind, be sober, and hope to the

end for the grace that is to be brought unto you at the revelation of Jesus Christ.

Many nights, would find me downstairs, hugging my Bible and Sandy my Retriever, crying out to the Lord, what have I done? O Father forgive me a sinner, for having gotten myself into this situation.

I would escape to the trails with my dogs, singing to the Lord at the top of my voice, trying to still the fear in me…Little did I know that Mike was stalking me…When returning home, Mike said to me, "you know, I can see you, but you will not be able to see me. Wherever you go, I will be watching you."

When I went to get groceries, he always had to come and would follow me around the store wearing his heavy boots, stomping them on the floor with each step. So much fear was building up in me…However, when it came to my dogs, if I heard any of them cry out in pain, I would be on him like a ton of bricks, all fear would be gone of him, I didn't care about myself, however, I warned him if I ever caught him hurting my dogs, he would be out of the house for good…

We had been married if you can call it that for almost ten months. Mike had gone down to Halifax to see his friends for the weekend and was coming back on Monday…I took this time to spend with the Lord, crying out to Him, "Father, what can I do?"…Then a Still Small Voice, said to me…" look in the bottom drawer of Mike's filing cabinet"…I said, "O Lord, I'm afraid to look, the Still Small Voice beckoned to me again, "Go and look, you will see what you need to know"…I went and gingerly looked…there were files, and as I went through them, I came to this file…"O dear Father, O no"…I felt sick, dirty, that Mike had ever touched me, and the acute realization of whom I had been married to. Mike was a Pedophile who had been to prison for the sexual molestation of young girls, along with his daughter. The horror was magnifying in me. I wrapped my arms around myself and howled in agony. How do I get out of this?

Suddenly realizing that the phone was ringing, I answered it. It was my neighbor, she said, "whatever is the matter, I'll be right over." Apparently, everyone in the neighborhood knew about Mike, as his picture had been in the newspapers when he was arrested by the RCMP upon the arrival back to his barracks in Winnipeg from tour duty. All my neighbors thought I had known about Mike, which of course I hadn't. Now, everything started to make sense.

Every Monday night, I had a care-group in my home, where we studied the Bible and sang hymns. This Monday, my neighbor had me come back to her home with her and await Mike's return from Halifax. Next Angela phoned the care group to meet at her house and explained what had happened.

When Mike came back from Halifax and found that I was not home, neither were the dogs.

He phoned Angela's home and asked if I was there. He told her to tell me to come home at once. When I didn't, he drove to the neighbors in a mad rush, stormed out of the car and demanded that I get in the car. I refused...instead, I told him to pack his bags and get out, and not to come back. He was so angry, his acerbity was awful, I started to cower, however, the care-group was there and they surrounded me and told him to go and pack his bags and that he would be given thirty minutes to get out, if he wasn't out by then they were going to call the police.

Angela's husband Bob who worked in a hardware store said that he was going to change all the locks in the house, in case Mike came back that night.

Then a few days later, I started receiving threatening phone calls from Mike, so I called the police, who also were aware of him...They started a report on Mike. Then Mike phoned to say that it didn't matter about the locks being changed, as he knew every square inch of the house, and that he could get in if he wanted to. Not only did he keep phoning me, but I started to receive letters from him. In these letters, he stated that he had contacted my relatives and friends. He had our computer with all their address and phone numbers.

The police started to keep a watch on me and my property because of all the threats that I was receiving from Mikel. My doctor was relieved that Mike had gone as when we had been living together, I was always ending up in the hospital with severe panic attacks, The doctor said that he was sending me to Dartmouth to see a psychiatrist who deals with high anxiety and panic attacks.

The psychiatrist was such a kind man and helped me so much. This particular time on a visit to him, the psychiatrist was going into my past with Brian. As we talked about what had happened in the marriage, I became upset that the marriage to Brian and the circumstances that I found myself in changed me, I was not the same person that I once was, and just howled out, "O my sons, my sons," how I longed to hold them in my arms again. The psychiatrist moved his chair beside me and held my hand and talked gently to me until I had stopped crying. How I wished that I could block all that terrible time out. My sons to this day have never known what I went through with their father, they had told me once that Brian had called them together and gave his version of what went on in the marriage, however, I couldn't say anything. I never wanted to talk about it, it was too traumatizing.

One day on my visit with the psychiatrist I asked if he would mind reading some of the letters that I had received from Mike. I needed reassurance that I wasn't reading into them something that wasn't there. I was in such a state of mind. The psychiatrist started to read them, then looked at me and said, "this man is really evil...You Must, have a peace bond against him. He then wrote a letter for me to take to the court in Truro. I had by now found out that Mike had a probation officer and had found out the name of the officer. So, I informed my psychiatrist of this fact. He said to let the probation officer see these letters and then for the officer to give it to the prosecutor and one to be given to the judge on the court day. This I did, and a court date was given.

On the court date, I had friends go with me as my psychiatrist warned me not to travel to Truro alone, where Mike was living. My psychiatrist was really worried about my safety. The judge awarded me the Peace Bond, then asked me how long I wanted it for? I said, "can I have it forever?" No dear, but I will grant you the maximum, which is a year. This was 1997. One year later we were divorced. Nevertheless, this was not going to stop him from causing trouble for me.

> Psalm 31:7 and 24 I will be glad and rejoice in thy mercy: for thou hast considered my trouble; thou hast known my soul in adversities...24. Be of good courage, and He shall strengthen your heart, all ye that hope in the Lord.

CHAPTER 13

MORE TESTING

Determination and hope in the Lord started me off on a new life. I began to attend the Presbyterian church in the village where I lived and became involved with the Bible study there. There was going to be a change in my life now and a better life for my precious dogs who helped me through the trials and tribulations that I had been going through. Renovations were started on the house, I wanted to give it a new look and wipe away the ugliness of what had taken place inside the house…Even though I still lived with the fear of Mike, I refused to allow my fears to take me captive. I knew without a doubt that Jesus was with me and knew He would never leave me or forsake me.

1998 I started to rescue Siberian Huskies, these beautiful dogs who are so loving, but were needlessly neglected and ill-treated, came to live with me. Sandy my retriever and Mickey my shepherd, now had two companions. A beautiful white Sibe named Anika and Tovia a sandy/white Sibe. These two beautiful Siberian Huskies would start me on a new beginning of rescuing these beautiful dogs. This would be even unto this day that I am writing my story. These dogs would always have a big part in my life.

When I was a teenager, I use to love ice skating. I would go to the large arena in Southampton, in the UK, where I grew up. I would lose myself in the music and just skate to my heart's content. Thinking about this, I went off and bought myself a pair of skates in the second-hand store in the village, then off I went to the village arena, happy at the prospect of skating again. It had been around thirty-odd years since I last skated. Arriving at the arena, and hearing the music, I fastened on my skates and off I went on the ice. How lovely to be skating again and to feel free as a bird. I was just getting into the rhythm...Bang, what was that noise? Why does my head hurt so badly? I had fallen back on my head and was lying there semi-conscious. I could hear voices around me but couldn't focus on anything or anyone. Next, I was being lifted into an ambulance, then the pain, I wish it would stop. Still in an out of consciousness, my doctor was speaking to me, but I couldn't say anything, and he was in and out of my vision. Then a long and agonizing trip down to Halifax. Another serious head injury...

In the year 2000, I had ordered a new Windstar van from the Ford Dealership in the village. So that I would have room for my dogs. After picking up the van, I went and picked up my girlfriend to take her out for lunch to celebrate getting my van. We had a lot in common, with our love for dogs. My friend was a Labrador breeder and had her own kennels. After dropping her back at home that afternoon, I decided to take a back road into the village, as there were a lot of potholes in the road that we had traveled on. Going along the road near the river, I rounded a corner, I was suddenly hitting washboard on the road, so went to apply a little pressure on my brakes but nothing happened, my brakes failed me. "Dear Father, what is happening?" I cried out to Him, the van rolled down into a ditch, apparently rolled over and started to roll towards the river, thankfully stopped just short of it. My plumber had seen what had happened and called the ambulance and fire department. When they came, they had to use the jaws of life to get to me. I had sustained another head and back injury again. My doctor sent me straight down to the Halifax Infirmary.

After a few months, I was able to get by with the help of a walker that my neighbor brought to me. Unfortunately, this was going to be another long process of healing.

> Joshua 1:9 Have not I commanded thee? Be strong, and of good courage, be not afraid, neither be thou dismayed. For the Lord, thy God is with thee, withersoever thou goest.

CHAPTER 14

HEAVEN SENT ESTATE FOR DOGS

A year later, I started a kennel called the (Heaven Sent Estate for Dogs). My neighbors helped me put up a wild animal fencing around the whole area at the back of the house. And a door was put into the back of the house so that the dogs and I would have easy access so that they could come and go freely. My vet knew I rescued Siberians and would call me if he had a husky brought into him in need of a home. I would travel down to pick the husky up and bring him/her to their new home. In time I ended up with seven of these beautiful creatures. These beautiful Sibes were such wonderful companions. Mickey my shepherd had died by this time, however, I still had Sandy, and would have her for another couple of years. Every day we would go and walk the trails together, I felt truly blessed by the Lord.

Sometime later, I had arranged with the pastor of my church to start a care group, similar to the one I had before, where we would meet, sing worship songs, study the Bible and have discussions on whatever topic we were studying. We again met every Monday; it was a great success. With people from the neighborhood and village, there were usually around twenty people. It was a lovely time together. After the meeting, we would socialize together and have refreshments.

It was during this time that I had a small job, working for the Humane Society, selling dog licenses. I would use this time meeting with people and telling them what the Lord had done in my life. I got to meet a lot of people during this time, it was quite lovely. On one of my calls, it was to a man with a dog, who invited me in for a cup of tea and as we talked, I could tell he was very lonely, his name was Doug. I invited him to come along to one of our Monday meetings, which he did. It was through these meetings that I found out that he was out of work. So, I asked him if he would like to do odd jobs for me? This he very much appreciated.

One day when he came round to work for me, he asked me if I would cut his hair for him, (he had long blond hair), so I said I would, But, I would have a chair outside, as I wasn't going to have him in the house with his shirt off. So, I started to cut his hair for him, I prayed quietly, asking the Lord to guide my words, while Doug was under the scissors. I thought to myself, he is going to hear the Gospel of our Lord. Whenever Doug started to question or argue about what I was saying, I would say he had better be careful, or his ear might get snipped by mistake. This led to Doug attending the church that I went to. I invited him to get involved with the Bible studies at the church, which he did, and quite enjoyed.

Doug and I became good friends, he would help me out on the property, and help me walk the dogs. It was a good relationship, good conversation and just enjoying each other's company, which was something new in my life which I hadn't quite experienced before.

One day Diane, Doug's sister came to visit me, while she was there, she said to me, "It is obvious that you and Doug are in love, instead of living separately, why don't you get married?" Doug's sister and family were lovely people and I enjoyed their company, I wasn't sure that I ever wanted to get married again. I decided to go and speak to the pastor with Doug. We were married under the apple tree with his family around us several months later.

Did I take this to the Lord? I'm not sure that I did. All I thought about during this time, was that I was loved for myself, by someone whom I could share the love of the Lord with and have a conversation with, without being put down, plus we were comfortable in each other's company. This was something I had always wanted. I had never been romanced before; it was wonderful.

We had been married for over a year, unfortunately, Doug was in and out of work, I couldn't understand this, as he seemed a good worker. It was during this time, that I was in the bathroom off the kitchen when I heard shouting going on. I went to investigate, Doug was at the sink washing up and yelling out to me, that he heard me talking about him in the bathroom. "I said, but there is no one in the house but us and the dogs." Again, he shouted at me and started coming towards me with malice on his face. I screamed and went running in the living room when suddenly I suffered a severe panic attack and collapsed. I came to and saw Doug's dad sitting in the armchair looking at me. Doug was back to his normal loving self. Confused, I looked at his dad, "what happened?" His dad said, "didn't Doug tell you?" "Tell me what, I asked?" His dad said, "Doug has Schizophrenia, is he off his medication?" "What medication?" I asked, well this was a shock, I had no idea, yes, he had funny moods now and again, but I left him to it, Schizophrenia? O no.

This explained the problem of not keeping his jobs. However, I loved Doug and was determined to try and help him, with the help of our doctor. The medications really messed him up. I knew Doug loved me and I felt bad for him. I wanted to help him in any way I could.

> Romans 8: 15 and 28 For ye have not received the spirit of bondage again to fear, but ye have received the Spirit of Adoption, whereby we cry Abba Father. 28. And we know that all things work together for good to them that love God, to them who are called according to His purpose.

We had been married for almost 4 years and during this time my Golden Retriever, Sandy had to be put to sleep, cancer had got the better of her. I mourned that dog; we had been through so much together. I was left with Sheiko, Blue, Anika, and Buddy.

I had been to see the bank manager about re-mortgaging the house, they had agreed to this to help me pay the bills, as Doug was rarely working, and my disability income wasn't enough.

We had been to church this particular Sunday and were invited back to friends for lunch. We had just finished lunch when I wasn't feeling too well, I knew something wasn't right with me. I said to Doug, "I think you had better take me home, I'm not feeling very well." So, making our excuses, we left. Getting into the car, I said to Doug, "you had better take me to the hospital instead, something is very wrong with me." Our doctor arrived at the hospital and as he examined me, touching my upper stomach, I screamed out in agony. The doctor went straight to the phone and called the surgeon on call in Amherst Hospital, then arranged speedy transport by ambulance to get me to the hospital. The pain was getting worse. Upon arrival in Amherst, the surgeon examined me and had an Xray taken, to find out that my Gall Bladder had burst and that crystals were going through my system.

I was immediately taken to the operating theatre and after a long operation, the surgeon came to see me, and said, "you, were a very lucky young lady, you almost died, however, you are not out of danger yet, as your body is septic." Nevertheless, I knew my God oversaw me and I was at peace.

During my long stay in the hospital, Doug came in with papers for me to sign from the bank, I wasn't very coherent, in that my awareness of what I was signing was not clear to me, however, Doug insisted that I sign them saying the bank needed them. Therefore, it was a shock to me when the bank phoned to say that Doug was drawing a lot of money out of the account. I said, "how can that be, we do not have a joint account?" "Actually, you do," said the manager, "that was among the papers that you signed."

CHAPTER 15

DISASTER

I arrived home at Christmas, still not well and in recovery mode. I was lying on the couch when Doug said, "I'll put more logs in the woodstove," I said, "no Doug, it's fine as it is," but he wouldn't listen to me. Next, a mighty roar as the chimney caught fire. "O dear Father, not anymore please?" Firemen came rushing in and said that the roof was on fire. I was half carried and dragged to our next-door neighbors about 50 yards away. It took the firemen a long time to contain the fire. The force of it had melted the woodstove, the room was an absolute mess. Thank goodness the dogs were outside and were safe.

Thankfully I had insurance, which covered a new roof, a new wood stove, the cleaning, and painting, plus a new carpet. It was never as nice as it had been. Through this time, I was in a lot of pain physically from the operation and had a huge scar. Plus, the recovery from the Sepsis. I was mentally and physically drained. "O Father, I need your guidance and your healing hand, please help me?"

> James 1:5 If any of you lack wisdom, let him ask of God,
> that giveth to all men liberally, and upbraideth not, and
> it shall be given him.

Later that year, money wasn't coming in from Doug, as he was out of work again, so I had no help with the bills. I would buy groceries for a month; however, Doug would eat them up in a week. One evening, sat in the living room with him and going over the bills in the ledger that I kept, I said to Doug, "we cannot go on like this, please stop taking food, as if it was going out of style, we cannot afford it, I am having a hard time making ends meet to pay all the bills." Looking at Doug, I could see his countenance change, so putting away the ledger, I said, "I am going to get ready for bed, as it was getting late in the evening.

I was in the bathroom to get ready for bed and had to go to the toilet, as I sat there, a sudden smash at the door of the bathroom and it burst open, in came Doug looking twice his size and blown up like a maniac. He started yelling at me saying I was talking about him again, then started hitting me around the face and head. Next, he picked me up and dragged me into the kitchen and threw me against the wall, beating on me the whole time. He opened the kitchen door and threw me down the stairs to the back door, continually hitting and yelling at me. Opened the back door and threw me into the driveway, next he flung the car keys at me and told me to get out and never to come back. Buddy the puppy came out to me as I scrambled to escape. I had been screaming for help, but nobody came. Getting into the car with Buddy, I drove to the neighbors next door, but nobody answered. Terrified, I cried out to the Lord, "Father, help me, what am I going to do? Suddenly the Still Small Voice said, "go to the police station in the village, there you will find a phone outside on the wall, pick it up and cry for help." By this time, I was in hysterics, I had never driven so fast, terrified of what Doug might do.

At the police station, taking Buddy with me to call for help, I picked up the phone, there was a policewoman at the other end, I told her what had happened. She said, "go back in your car and lock the doors and that a police cruiser would be there shortly." It seemed like an eternity. I was hurting so badly and couldn't stop shaking. Then lights shining on my car as the police cruiser came alongside my car. The officers took me to the hospital where I was treated and stayed with me. The doctor said to me, "I'm sorry but we have no beds left for you to be able to stay here. I said, "I have a puppy in the car that will need me, what am I going to do? I'll have to sleep in the car with the dog." The police officer said, "don't worry, we are going over to your house to arrest Doug, and taking him down to Bible Hill station, he won't be bothering you." A while later an officer came to the hospital to tell me that Doug had been arrested and taken off to Bible

Hill prison and that I will be safe at home and tomorrow the officers will come by to see me and let me know what will take place. So, after a while, still terrified I was able to drive home with Buddy.

During the next weeks, going through notes in the house, I realized that Mike and Doug knew each other. This really threw me for a loop, how on earth could this happen. Then realizing Mike's cunning ways, I knew this was possible.

Then my friend received a call from Mike, saying that he was going to blow up the house I lived in. So, Gwen contacted the police and informed them of the phone call. Then more death threats followed. The police were very helpful and had known of Mike and Doug's alliance, so they agreed to give me police protection and would keep an eye on my home and property. This was a very scary time; little did I comprehend the fact that I would be under police protection until I left Canada.

Letters from the bank started arriving, asking me to pay back on my mortgage. I had been trying to pay down on all the bills, but my disability payments were not enough to cover all the bills that came in. I found an auctioneer and asked him to come out and value all my furnishings and valuables that I had. When the auctioneer came out, he went through all the house, as I had some lovely Colonial furniture. He said he would give me $7,000.00 for everything and arranged to come out with a truck to pick everything up. This left me with no beds or bedroom furniture, no table or chairs, or living room, dining room or kitchen furniture, except my old couch and armchair that the auctioneer said was not worth anything. This helped me pay off some of my depts.

Of a nighttime, I would put a comforter and pillows on the floor and lay down with my dogs to sleep.

Finally, I sought money counseling and met with a very kind man who advised me that I would not be able to pay the bills as I had insufficient income to do so. The counselor put me in touch with a private trustee who would take care of me for the next seven years. "O Father, not again, not another bankruptcy, what was I going to do, and where could I possibly go?"

My lawyer in the meantime had written to the government with papers to get my name changed. The name change arrived a month later.

> Colossians 1:23 If ye continue in the faith grounded and settled and be not moved away from the hope of the gospel, which ye have heard.......

I started 3 days of silent praying and reading and meditating on the Word of God and making notes of what the Lord was putting on my mind. Where was I going to go? I asked myself. I started driving around looking for places for the dogs and me to live, without any success Nevertheless, unbeknown to me the Lord was working on my behalf…

The following Sunday, while praying and crying out to the Lord, "where shall I go?" That Still Small Voice said to me, "phone Mary and Bill," these were my friends in Pugwash, Nova Scotia. "The Still Small Voice continued, they are wanting to sell their house, ask them if they would be willing to rent-to-own their house to you?" So I phoned Mary and Bill and said to Mary who answered the phone, "Mary, I have been praying, and the Lord has asked me to ask you, would you be willing to rent-to-own your house. Mary said, "let me ask Bill, I'll phone you back." Less than 5 minutes later, the phone rang. Mary said, "How does $400 a month sound to you?" Then Mary said, "Bill has been wanting to move down to Amherst, however, we haven't been able to sell the house." "Praise the Lord, Hallelujah to my God." Bill and Mary moved me in that Friday, they had already rented an apartment in Amherst and had moved in. Through the help of the trustee, I was able to build up my credit again, and eventually purchased the house in Pugwash, some years later.

> Psalm 91:2 I will say of the Lord, He is my refuge and my fortress: My God in Him will I trust.

CHAPTER 16

A NEW JOURNEY

The year was 2005 and the house in Pugwash was very small in comparison to my last house, however, I was blessed by what the Lord had done for me. Determined to make it as cozy as I possibly could. I just felt so blessed with the way the Lord had provided for me. My heart and mind were filled with praise for my Lord Jesus, I was so overjoyed by His faith in me, a sinner.

I had bought with me some of the wild animal fencings and posts. The fencing I put up first to take care of the dogs and keep them safe. They had a good area to play in which pleased me very much.

I was still sleeping on the floor with the dogs as I didn't have a bed or furniture, except for my old armchair. I remembered my funeral plan that I had put in place early in my arrival in Nova Scotia. So, I phoned the funeral home to see if I was able to cancel it and receive my money back? Yes, they could refund the money for me, "thank you, Lord," this would help me to get some furnishings. My friends found a bed put out for collection and brought it to me, after cleaning it up, the bed came out perfect. I just needed a mattress to go on it, this I found in a sale. Finally, I had a bed to sleep in again.

On my street was a Baptist church that I started to attend and eventually was asked to join the choir. This I loved and made some good friends during this time. The pastor had teamed me up with a lady in the choir, Sheila, she was lovely, and we became firm friends. Unfortunately, a couple of years later Sheila became ill and died. I missed this dear friend very much. As time went on, I felt something was missing in the church,

I was so hungry for the Word of God. It was during this time while at the hospital in Pugwash for an Xray, that I met a certain Xray technician whose name was Laurie, who was always preaching the gospel, it didn't matter who was there, Laurie would quote the gospel. I knew Laurie was a Seventh Day Adventist and found out his last name and decided to phone him and his wife at their home. When speaking to Bev, Laurie's wife, I asked if I could go to their church. They said, yes, in fact, they would pick me up on Saturday to take me to church. This started me off on a wonderful journey with my Lord, plus Laurie and Bev became fast firm friends who I would go to church with every Saturday. I loved the teaching and the love that was in the church. 2009 I was baptized and have never looked back. Jesus became my husband who loves me unconditionally and is my forever friend.

These wonderful people at this church helped me so much. And did so much for me. They knew from Laurie that I had left some things at my previous house and said that they would take me over in a large van to collect the items that I had left behind. I made inquiries and received permission to go and pick up the items, as the house had not been sold yet. They brought everything back for me, including my old couch and stove.

I started to renovate the house in Pugwash myself but was having a hard time with it as I only had a few tools. Laurie came by one day with another member and saw what I was trying to do. "You cannot do that," said Laurie, "leave it and I will come with some of the men and we will take care of this for you." Which they did, they drywalled the bedroom and where I was trying to seal up a door, one of the men built me a bookcase to go in where the door was. They built a closet that I had tried to build with no success. They did a wonderful job for me, with no charge! Later on, Laurie with the aid of John another member of the church, purchased and put in a stainless- steel flue piping and connected it to my stove, so that I could have a fire and be warm. Again, they would not accept any payment for what they had bought and built for me.

During this time that the men were coming in to do the work, I started to feel overwhelmed and had a hard time trying to deal with it all. Never before had this kind of goodwill ever been given or shown towards me by man. It affected me a great deal, I was deeply shaken that mankind could ever be this way with me. This was totally foreign to me, even now typing this out, I can feel and experience what I went through. Feeling such worthlessness and wretched as a dirty rag doll. I hadn't met this kindness in mankind before. I also had another very dear friend from the church, Miriam whom I had sat with at church, she was so kind and loving and because of my interest in Ellen G. White, had given me books of hers, as she had duplicate copies that members of her family had bought. I felt so blessed about this and have come to love her writings. I had many dear and wonderful friends at this church, they were a real blessing.

When first coming to Pugwash, I had gone to see the Postmistress at the Post office to let her know about my circumstances, in case Mike should turn up and want some information about me. Apparently, he had been there, however, they are not allowed to give out information on anyone, which I was so relieved about. Mike had found out somehow that I was in Pugwash but didn't know where. The Pugwash police knew about my circumstances and were aware of Mike. Then letters started being left at the post office for me by Mike, these I took to the police, who said, I would need another Peace Bond and would have to go to Amherst to apply for one. I didn't want to see him again; I couldn't deal with that.

My precious dogs that I had brought with me, my beautiful Anika, a pure white Siberian, Sheiko, he was so precious to me and knew how much he was loved, Blue, a shiny dark black with piercing blue eyes, he was a loveable rascal and my Buddy, who was a mixed Siberian/Lab. We had so much fun together, taking them down to the beach for long walks and play in the water. How I loved my dogs. One day, I went out to the deck at the back of the house and Anika had bitten into her shoulder where a lump had suddenly appeared, and she was bleeding quite badly. I rushed over to my neighbor and asked, "would you run me to the vets as something is terribly wrong with Anika?" This he did, and I sat at the back of the truck with Anika with a large towel around her. Arriving at the vets, they took her in straight away. I sat there crying wondering what had happened. I didn't have too much faith in these new vets. White later, they came out to me, they couldn't save Anika a blood vessel had been severed. I was mortified, Anika dead she was only eight years old, this precious little girl of mine. I just couldn't be consoled. Back at home, I just sat on the floor with Sheiko, Blue and Buddy, hugged them to me and cried. Huskies are very sensitive to their owner's feelings.

During the summer while working in the garden, I had to go to the shed for a tool, as I was coming out of the shed, my laces caught on a tine by the door, and I fell flat on my face on the concrete path. I screamed out for help, then unconsciousness. Next thing I knew, I was being lifted onto a stretcher with a brace around my neck and back brace then rushed off to the hospital. Another head and back injury.

According to my neighbors afterward, the police came flying down thinking that Mike had attacked me. It was the police who ordered the ambulance men to put me onto a brace. My face ended up all the colors of the rainbow, it was a wonder that I hadn't broken any bones.

Again, it took a while for healing to be accomplished, however, with the help of the Lord, He again renewed me, and my strength was back. It was during this time, one night, that my Sheiko took to having seizures, I laid with him comforting him and praying over him. He went back to sleep, however, in the morning out in the garden, I noticed that he had fallen over. I ran out to him and found he was having more seizures. I phoned the vets that I now had and told them and said I was bringing Sheiko down to them. With the help of a neighbor, we put a blanket under Sheiko to lift him into my car. We were only half an hour away from home, when he started having another seizure. I stopped the car and went to him, however, he died in my arms. He was such a precious boy. I turned the car around and drove back home and buried him alongside of Anika in the garden. A year later I was to lose Blue and Buddy. This was so hard to overcome. Nevertheless, I went and rescued a beautiful black and white Siberian and named her Anika, she was so precious and would follow me everywhere.

CHAPTER 17

A NEW LIFE

The year was 2013 and my uncle in England phoned and asked me if I would like to come for a visit to England and to bring my mother who now lived in Niagara Falls? He asked me to arrange everything and would send me the money, which he did. I contacted my mother and told her what her brother had said to me about going to visit him. She was very excited about it and said she would arrange with a friend of hers to drive her to Toronto Airport where we would meet to fly to England. During our visit with my uncle, he asked my mother, "was she happy where she was living, or is there a place she would like to move in to"? Mom said that a friend of hers had moved into this certain retirement home for seniors and said how lovely it was. Mom gave the name of the place and I brought it up on my uncles' computer. It certainly was beautiful inside to look at, and, as my uncle read through what they had to offer, he said to mom, would you like to move in there? Well, of course, she would, there was no question about it. I then contacted the retirement home and spoke to the manager there and asked if there were any vacancies? Yes, there was, so I arranged with the manager to e-mail the forms necessary to get mom moved in as soon as possible. We had a wonderful time with my uncle, seeing my cousins and visiting with my brother who now lived in Wales.

Back at home in Nova Scotia, I made arrangements with my bank to set up a special account, so that my uncle could wire the money over to pay the rent for my mom. She is still there to this day, in her late nineties, however, she has become very feeble and her memory is failing her.

2014 came, and again my uncle phoned to ask me if I wanted to come for another visit in the summer, and to bring mom along? Again, he asked me to arrange everything, only this time to use the money in the account to pay for the travel arrangements. It was wonderful to see my uncle and cousins again. While at his hotel in the New Forest, my uncle asked me, "would I like to come back to the UK to live?" I said, "that is my prayer and dream to come back, I had been wanting to leave Canada for some time." Five minutes later, he looked at me, and said, "would you really like to come back?" I said, "yes, but I couldn't possibly afford to buy a home in the UK." "Don't you worry," he said to me, "I will buy you a house to live in, where would you like to live?" I just gasped, my uncle would buy me a house, O Father, how wonderful, I thought to myself. I was absolutely stunned at the thought of leaving all the misery I had experienced in Canada behind.

The next day, my uncle took mom and me down to Pembrokeshire, where my brother lives. I said to Laurie, "I'm coming back here to live." He gave me a great big hug. I said to my uncle and brother, "first, we must find my church, then my house. So, Laurie went onto the internet and brought up the Seventh Day Adventist Church in Carmarthen. I was so excited, my uncle said he would take me down to see it. I was so full of gratitude to the Lord for what He was doing for me. I realized that the Lord was using my uncle as His tool to get things completed in the way He wanted. The church was very old and very Welsh, the whole setting around the church was so scenic, with a rushing brook to one side and lovely old trees around.

By the time we arrived back at my brothers', Laurie had found a bungalow in a very old Welsh village high up on a hill in Carmarthenshire. It was beautiful and my uncle said, "I like the look of it, this is just what you need, I'm going to put in an offer." My eyes just about popped out of my head, when I saw it, it was so beautiful with lots of gardens, which I love and out in the countryside which I needed. My uncle, needless to say, is a very generous man and always has been, and of whom I shall always be grateful.

My Father in heaven, You are so faithful to me, thank you for your endless mercy that you show towards me.

I arrived back in Pugwash, Nova Scotia towards the end of July 2014. The houses in Pugwash were not selling and those that did sell were selling at a loss. Nevertheless, I knew that God was in control of this whole situation, so I put my trust in Him completely.

The first Realtor I quickly fired, realizing that he was not working for my best interest. Next, I asked a friend if he would look after the sale of my house. This worked out well. He had many people come through the home. During this time, I had such a strong feeling that the house would be sold and that I would be back in England again this year. With that in mind, I started to pack and box items that I would need to send over to England. Then one day, this lady had an appointment to came through the house and she spent a lot of time in the gardens that I had created with the help and guidance of the Lord, everything was organic. Strawberries, raspberries, blackberries I had in the plenty. Gardens of beautiful roses and flowering shrubs. It had been a work of love. This lady wandered around, then came in and sank into my armchair, she had such a look of peace about her. On talking to her, she said that she worked out on the oil fields in Alberta and was looking for a home to retire in. I really liked her and felt so strongly that this was going to be the buyer of my home.

The following day, my friend the Realtor, phoned me to say that he had an offer on the house, he didn't sound very upbeat, so I was surprised and delighted when he said that the offer at my house was $10,000.00 more than I had asked for. He said that the lady was taking all my furnishings and that the closing date was for October 23rd, 2014. This left me less than a month to get everything taken care of. However, I wasn't worried as I knew the Lord had everything in His control. The ladies Realtor came to see me and couldn't believe all that I was letting the lady have. Next, she said to me, what are you going to do about Anika your husky? With tears in my eyes, I said, I don't know, I explained how I had phoned the airport cargo to ask for the price of taking my dog. I said it would cost me $2,000.00, and I don't have that kind of money, as my uncle was taking care of the cost for the airline and he wasn't prepared to pay another $2,000.00 for Anika.

Later that day, I received a phone call from the lady's Realtor to tell me that $2,000.00 is being posted into your bank for you to take Anika with you. I couldn't believe the generosity of the lady. Overjoyed, I praised the Lord, thanking Him for what He was doing, got on the floor and hugged Anika, saying you are coming with me, tears of joy were in my eyes. I thought what do I need to do. I phoned the vets and told them about the situation. They would prepare the papers for Anika and would make an appointment for me and Anika to see the government vet in Moncton, New Brunswick. Then I had to apply for a pet passport for Anika. This was a very crazy and exciting time. The airline had been booked, including my transfer plane in Toronto. The $2,000.00 was in my bank, so I contacted cargo at the airport to book Anika in giving them my flight number and times. They told me the size of the crate I was to buy for Anika and what to put in it.

On the 23rd, October, I had an appointment with my lawyer for the closing day of the house. I also had to travel to Moncton with Anika to see the Government Vet. Anika was stamped and cleared so that she wouldn't have to go into quarantine. Then off to the pet store for her crate.

The 26th, October was the day Anika and I was to fly out. My dear friends, Laurie, Bev and Gilbert were going to be driving Anika and me to Halifax International Airport. First to take Anika to the cargo area where she would be put into her crate and all her papers checked. Well, we had a problem, the crate I was told to buy, was too small, they would not allow her to go on the plane in the one I had bought. What was I to do? You still have time to go to the mall and buy a larger one, I was told. Gilbert stayed with Bev and Laurie drove me to the pet shop, where I purchased a larger crate. Then back to cargo to assemble it. This was done, Anika was on her way.

Arriving at departures with my friends, I was told my luggage was too heavy, I would either have to leave one behind or go to the shop in the airport to purchase a new piece of luggage. This I did, oh what a fiasco I had in the middle of the floor transferring clothing out of one case into the new, underwear and all sorts were falling on the ground in my panic to get things sorted out. Finally, all was done, and I said my goodbyes to my dear friends and got ready to board the plane.

However, this isn't all that happened. The devil was having fun with me. He was not at all happy the way things were turning out for me. There was going to be a surprise waiting for me at Heathrow Airport. Upon arrival at Heathrow, going to customs, even though I had my UK passport and papers, they said they had no record of me, and that I had to go and sit in the guarded area until I was cleared. O dear Father now what? I know that you are in charge,

> Deuteronomy 31:6 Be strong and of a good courage, fear not, nor be afraid of them: for the Lord thy God, He it is that doth go with thee; He will not fail thee, nor forsake thee.

One hour later, the officer came up to me and apologized, saying that they couldn't find me in the records, however, after speaking to the head office, they are relinquishing me and that I was free to go. Thank you, Father. Looking around everyone had gone, I thought where is my luggage? There it was put up against a post, then I spotted a porter and asked if he could take me to the entrance, which he did. There were my poor uncle and cousin waiting for me. O what a joyous reunion. Now to go and collect Anika. It took only ten minutes before she came out, then we were on our way home. Praise the Lord, Hallelujah!!

During the next months, I spent with my uncle in his beautiful home. Anika playing with Digby my uncles' Labrador on his lovely estate. There were 3 acres of lovely grounds that his large bungalow stood on. I was very happy there with my uncle, spending time with him. Unfortunately, his younger son was causing a lot of problems for him, on one of these occasions, he attacked my uncle, thank goodness I was there to go in-between them and to be able to call the ambulance and the police. My uncle was badly shaken up; however, his son had taken off for the train station to get to him back home.

Having watched my young cousin during the time I was there, he was showing all the same signs and symptoms that my husband Doug had shown with schizophrenia. I never knew if my cousin had been tested for this or not, nevertheless, my cousin was to prove to be very vindictive over the years to come to every member of the family. Unfortunately, my cousin was a loose cannon.

January 2015, I was finally able to see my new home in Wales. Tears came into my eyes as we traveled through Wales to my home, it was so beautiful, the countryside, hills, and valleys were magnificent. Upon seeing my home, I couldn't believe it, it was far better than I had imagined.

The home was so lovely and the view from the back of the house, looked out onto hills, valleys and the sea. I couldn't believe this was going to be my home for the rest of my life. "Oh, Father, You knew exactly what I was needing, the scenery. The peace and quiet of the countryside, beautiful gardens for me to work in. Thank You, so much for bringing me here," I prayed.

In February, I rescued a lovely Labrador/retriever, called Bailey who was to prove to be a wonderful companion not only for Anika but for myself too. How they loved each other, Bailey would fuss over Anika looking after her. The joy it gave me to see them run and play. I was so very happy.

In my church, I was taking on responsibilities that I hadn't had back in Canada. One day, I was asked by the head elder, "would I like to take a Lay Preaching course in Cardiff?" Oh, yes, please. I knew the Lord was leading me in this way. The course was fantastic, I didn't want it to stop, but unfortunately, it had to. I received my Lay Preaching credentials, what a wonderful feeling. "Lord, you lead me in this," I prayed. "What do you want my first sermon to be about I asked? the Still Small Voice came to me quite distinctively. "You must give your testimony first." "O Lord," I said, "I cannot talk in church about my upbringing or my first marriage, it was too awful." Again, the Still Small Voice spoke unto me, "Then, you must write a book on your life and how I have helped you."

This was two years ago, and constant prodding's by the Lord, that has taken me since then to be able to write this book. October 2019 was when I first started. My holy family, Father, Son and the Holy Spirit have guided me every step of the way. They have known the agonizing periods of writing this book, however, without their help and guidance, this book wouldn't have been written. I give all Praise, Honor and Glory to my precious holy family.

The year was 2019, Anika my little girl was ill and having to have a lot of treatments from the vets. I prayed, "Jesus, I don't want too be without a Siberian in my life, these dogs are so precious to me. Do you think I should get another Siberian already?" I looked on the husky rescue site and applied for a husky, they were not very forthcoming, so I went back and prayed again, "Jesus show me what to do." Right at that moment of prayer, the Lord put upon my heart, (Many Tears Rescue). I went and looked on their site and right there was Blusie, a large black and white Siberian, I thought dear Lord, You knew. I applied for Blusie and within two weeks she was home with us. What a beautiful gentle creature she is, while Anika was alive, Blusie would lie down beside her, I know she sensed how ill she was, two months later, it was Anika's time to take her to the vets, she was too precious to me to let her suffer, Anika had been such a faithful companion. Now I have this again with Blusie and Bailey.

Our dear Lord and Savior know of all the hurting, aching hearts, and souls out there. What my Lord and Savior has done for me, He can do for you too, if only you will trust and believe in Him. If you do, like me, you will never look back. Go forward with our dear Lord and Savior, He is holding out His hand for you to grab hold of. With the help of Jesus, you can learn to forgive those who have hurt and abused you in your life. When I was able to do this, I was set free, no more bitterness, no more grief. Let our precious Savior help you and you too will be set free.

Remember always, Jesus loves you, you are loved by a wonderful compassionate Savior.

> Matthew 11:28 Come unto me, all ye that labor and are heavy laden, and I will give you rest.
>
> Proverbs 3: 5-6 Trust in the Lord with all thine heart; and lean not unto thine own understanding, in all your ways acknowledge Him, and He shall direct your path.

www.ingramcontent.com/pod-product-compliance
Lightning Source LLC
Chambersburg PA
CBHW030159100526
44592CB00009B/358